CAMBRIDGE LIBRARY COLLECTION

Books of enduring scholarly value

Education

This series focuses on educational theory and practice, particularly in the context of eighteenth- and nineteenth-century Europe and its colonies, and America. During this period, the questions of who should be educated, to what age, to what standard and using what curriculum, were widely debated. The reform of schools and universities, the drive towards improving women's education, and the movement for free (or at least low-cost) schools for the poor were all major concerns both for governments and for society at large. The books selected for reissue in this series discuss key issues of their time, including the 'appropriate' levels of instruction for the children of the working classes, the emergence of adult education movements, and proposals for the higher education of women. They also cover topics that still resonate today, such as the nature of education, the role of universities in the diffusion of knowledge, and the involvement of religious groups in establishing and running schools.

The Conflict of Studies

The nineteenth century was a time of great reform in education, with debate focusing on such questions as who should be educated, in what manner, and to what degree. Given the technical advances brought about by the Industrial Revolution, rigorous mathematical education was seen by many as essential. A mathematician, educator and examiner for the University of Cambridge, Isaac Todhunter (1820–84) was also known as a prolific and very successful author of mathematics textbooks. In his day, he was considered an influential, albeit somewhat conservative, figure in mathematical education. In these six essays, first published in 1873, he discusses topics raised by the reform movement (for which he had little sympathy), such as the examination system, teaching methods and materials. Born of Todhunter's vast experience in the field, this work reflects an insider's perspective and remains relevant to students and scholars interested in the history of mathematics teaching and the University of Cambridge.

Cambridge University Press has long been a pioneer in the reissuing of out-of-print titles from its own backlist, producing digital reprints of books that are still sought after by scholars and students but could not be reprinted economically using traditional technology. The Cambridge Library Collection extends this activity to a wider range of books which are still of importance to researchers and professionals, either for the source material they contain, or as landmarks in the history of their academic discipline.

Drawing from the world-renowned collections in the Cambridge University Library and other partner libraries, and guided by the advice of experts in each subject area, Cambridge University Press is using state-of-the-art scanning machines in its own Printing House to capture the content of each book selected for inclusion. The files are processed to give a consistently clear, crisp image, and the books finished to the high quality standard for which the Press is recognised around the world. The latest print-on-demand technology ensures that the books will remain available indefinitely, and that orders for single or multiple copies can quickly be supplied.

The Cambridge Library Collection brings back to life books of enduring scholarly value (including out-of-copyright works originally issued by other publishers) across a wide range of disciplines in the humanities and social sciences and in science and technology.

The Conflict of Studies

*And Other Essays on Subjects
Connected with Education*

ISAAC TODHUNTER

CAMBRIDGE
UNIVERSITY PRESS

CAMBRIDGE UNIVERSITY PRESS

Cambridge, New York, Melbourne, Madrid, Cape Town,
Singapore, São Paolo, Delhi, Mexico City

Published in the United States of America by Cambridge University Press, New York

www.cambridge.org
Information on this title: www.cambridge.org/9781108059374

© in this compilation Cambridge University Press 2013

This edition first published 1873
This digitally printed version 2013

ISBN 978-1-108-05937-4 Paperback

THE CONFLICT OF STUDIES

AND OTHER ESSAYS.

𝔆𝔞𝔪𝔟𝔯𝔦𝔡𝔤𝔢:

PRINTED BY C. J. CLAY, M.A.

AT THE UNIVERSITY PRESS.

THE

CONFLICT OF STUDIES

AND OTHER ESSAYS

ON

SUBJECTS CONNECTED WITH EDUCATION.

BY

I. TODHUNTER, M.A., F.R.S.,

FORMERLY FELLOW AND PRINCIPAL MATHEMATICAL LECTURER
OF ST JOHN'S COLLEGE, CAMBRIDGE.

London:

MACMILLAN AND CO.

1873.

PREFACE.

So much discussion has occurred in recent years respecting the subjects to which this volume is devoted, that it must appear presumptuous to publish some new essays unless a reasonable claim can be established to that attention which they solicit. The writer may venture to state that he has enjoyed favourable opportunities for becoming practically acquainted with the matters on which he treats. A long residence at Cambridge, continued occupation in lecturing, much experience in examinations, both in the University and elsewhere, and a share in the deliberations of several important Syndicates which have been employed in the reconstruction of official courses of study — all these circumstances combined might be expected to induce and enable a person to form definite opinions on many points connected with the general subject of education. How far these advantages have been duly cultivated must be left for the reader to estimate.

It is then mainly on the ground of his own experience that the writer presumes to ask for the consideration of the conclusions at which he has arrived; and this leads him naturally to request indulgence for the form he has adopted in setting forth those conclusions. It will be seen that he has throughout referred to processes and facts which have fallen under his own observation; and that he has repeatedly expressed himself rather in the manner of a witness who is offering such evidence as he possesses than of an advocate who is arguing a cause, or of a judge who is pronouncing a decision. He trusts that this course, and the language which he has in consequence employed, will be attributed solely to his wish to accept the responsibility for his remarks, and not to an undue confidence in his own opinions. For the same reason his chief regard has been given to such points as seemed to have been altogether overlooked, or at least much neglected, in various former discussions; while those have been avoided which had already been adequately treated.

It was originally the writer's expectation that the Essays would have appeared separately in some magazine or review; but he has yielded to the suggestion that they might with convenience be collected into an independent volume. Occasionally a brief allusion will be found in one Essay to some topic which occurs also in another; this slight repetition

is owing to the mode of publication which was originally contemplated, and it is hoped will be readily
excused.

The Essays have been written at such scanty in-
tervals of leisure as other very laborious engagements
allowed, and have been substantially finished for many
months; but unavoidable delay has occurred in finally
arranging them for the press, so that they were not
placed in the hands of the publisher until the commencement of the present year. The last essay remains as it was written before the first examination
on the new system for the Mathematical Tripos had
taken place: and no remarks have been added to
shew how the anticipations expressed have been confirmed by the event.

While these sheets have been passing through
the press, some of the opinions to which the writer
attaches great weight have received important con-
firmation.

Thus on pages 19 and 20 attention has been invited
to the special value of training in exact science before
devotion to studies of a more popular kind; and the
following sentence in corroboration may be quoted from
an article on the late Professor Sedgwick by an eminent authority: "Pressed in early life through a strict
course of study, he found himself stronger by that
training than most of his fellow geologists, but never
made them feel his superiority."

On pages 147...152 the writer has undertaken to maintain the mathematical reputation of England in comparison with that of foreign countries, and he fears that this will at first sight appear paradoxical, so frequently is the contrary opinion either avowed or assumed. An interesting work, bearing on such a comparison, has recently been published by M. de Candolle at Geneva; and in a notice of it in the *Revue des Deux Mondes* for February, 1873, the high position of England is fully recognised: see especially page 731 of the Review. Almost immediately after the preceding sentence had been finished, the writer found in the *Contemporary Review* for March, 1873, a most able vindication of the conspicuous merit of England, both in science and philosophy, and among other references is one to the page above cited of the "leading French periodical."

On page 160 the writer has recorded his own testimony in opposition to the very disparaging statements which have recently been made as to the use of Euclid's Elements of Geometry; the report of the Cambridge Local Examinations Syndicate, just issued, speaks in extremely favourable terms of the attainments of the candidates in this subject, thus adding another to the numerous testimonies respecting the value of the well-known text-book.

Finally, the writer regrets to have observed very recently, in one of the most esteemed weekly newspapers, remarks like those which have often been made, but which are shewn to be untenable on pages 200 and 201 ; in this case they were indeed attributed to another paper, but they ought not to have been reproduced in a periodical of high reputation for character and intelligence. In the same place some numerical results as to marks were given, which were in direct opposition to the general statement made on page 208, and which, so far, were quite erroneous.

CAMBRIDGE, *March* 31, 1873.

CONTENTS.

		PAGE
I.	The Conflict of Studies	1
II.	Competitive Examinations	32
III.	Private Study of Mathematics	65
IV.	Academical Reform	104
V.	Elementary Geometry	136
VI.	The Mathematical Tripos	193

ESSAYS.

THE CONFLICT OF STUDIES.

IF we cast our eyes back for a period of fifty years we shall arrive at an epoch when the higher education of England remained still, as it had been for many generations, solely and exclusively classical. An illustrious man trained at this time stated in later life, with well-feigned regret, that he belonged to the pre-scientific period. Suddenly a strong current arose in favour of *useful knowledge;* the machinery of lectures, mechanics' institutions, and cheap literature, was employed for the diffusion of this useful knowledge among the humbler classes. Whatever might have been the result of these agencies within the sphere of their immediate operation, it cannot be said that any decisive influence was produced on the schools and colleges which supply the most elaborate education.

At a later period, when the machinery set in action for the benefit of the humbler classes had decayed in power, when mechanics' institutions had fallen into debt and difficulty, when lectures had given place to musical and other entertainments, when popular literature had ceased to affect to teach and aspired only to please, the exclusively classical education of the upper classes

T.   1

in England first encountered serious criticism. Perhaps not more than ten or twelve years have elapsed since these time-honoured studies began to experience any vigorous rivalry; though for a considerably longer period the elements of mathematics had gained a partial and temporary toleration.

I do not know that any single cause, or any combination of two or three definite causes, can be assigned with certainty as having led to the conflict of studies which we now propose to consider. As we proceed some suggestions will occur which may throw light on this matter; but I do not propose to discuss it formally. I do not pretend to exhaust the subject on which I write, but only to offer such remarks as have presented themselves to my own reflection, and so far as I know have not yet been brought prominently forward.

The first point to which I shall allude is one which seems to me commonly neglected, namely, that in balancing the claims of various modes of education and systems of studies we must remember that our decision must depend very much on the precise benefit which we hope to secure. We may propose to educate an individual mainly for his own benefit, or for that of others, as for instance the state. If we take the benefit of the state as the principal end we shall probably be led to the conclusion that the indications of any special excellence should be carefully watched and encouraged, even at the expense of the general development of the powers. If a youth shews any of the tastes and habits which have been in past time the presages of military distinction, we may hold that the law of the safety of the country justifies the cultivation of this

promise even to the neglect of higher intellectual qualities, or to the peril of moral excellence itself. This
may be an extreme case; but let us take a more moderate example. Suppose a youth to exhibit a fondness
for imaginative exercises and literature, which may be
the dawn of poetical genius. Moreover let us suppose
that, in spite of the authority of an ancient sage, we
find a function and a value for poets in our commonwealth; then we may conclude that we ought to stimu-
late the imagination: though perhaps it might be for
the true happiness of the individual if the memory and
the reason were trained rather than a faculty which is
already unduly developed. It is unnecessary to illustrate the matter further, for it is sufficiently obvious.
If we are merely pleasing our fancy with the construction of a Platonic republic we may determine that the
endowments of the individual belong strictly to the
state, and are to be developed and employed prima-
rily for the public benefit; and if we believe that history repeats itself we may anticipate that at some
future period the example of Sparta will be revived,
and individual and family life be subordinated to the
paramount claims of the commonwealth.

Probably however the end which is usually sought
is the good of the individual rather than of the state;
but our proceedings seem often ill-calculated to secure
the supposed end.

Although there may be little immediate prospect
of having such a control exercised by the state as to
involve the absolute command of all individual talent;
yet on some grounds at least we might long for such a
dispensation. How often do we see men eminently

qualified for some important work which they will not undertake; and then we may wish for some benevolent despotism to exert the necessary constraining authority. Here for instance is a philosopher who could supply us with a treatise on some difficult and important branch of science; there a scholar who could edit in a worthy manner the works of some great author: but philosopher and scholar alike neglect what seems to all others the obvious duty. Not only may we complain that those who possess such eminent endowments do not employ them; but we have the additional mortification of finding that those who could perform the required work well, though somewhat inferior to the great masters, are discouraged from attempting it by the conviction that at last their performance may be thrown into the shade by utterances from the oracles which have so long been dumb.

I wish that those who occupy the highest places in professional science and learning would sometimes reflect on the fact that their eminence may be really an obstacle to the progress of knowledge if they communicate little or nothing themselves: for their reputation naturally deters others from attempting to produce works on the appropriated subjects.

Although we have no such despotic power as to compel an individual to cultivate just that faculty which seems strongest, yet by our system of competitive examinations and prizes we tend to the same result. We take a boy at school who seems to exhibit an aptitude, say for mathematics, and foster that taste in every way we can. The boy comes to the University; he is already saturated with mathematics, and so must have almost exhausted the special benefit which that study is held to confer: at the same time in other departments of knowledge, such as languages, history, natural science, he may be very deficient. Nevertheless he is kept for three or more years still at the old pursuits, exercising only those energies which have been abundantly developed, and leaving others dormant which have been too long neglected. If our object is to train mathematical teachers and professors this may be defended, though perhaps with only partial success; but if, as we commonly maintain, our object is to cultivate the mind so as to render it well fitted for future exertion in any direction which has to be followed, our arrangements are open to serious doubts.

The excessive cultivation for examination purposes of one department of knowledge to the exclusion of others seems to me one of the great evils of our modern system of bribing students by great prizes and rewards to go through our competitive struggles. We are in danger of giving up all pretence of a general course of training for youth, and of allowing and even encouraging boys to select some special subject which they fancy they prefer, or rather perhaps which they least dislike. I should desire quite a contrary system; a scheme of study and examination should be drawn up after due deliberation, and all candidates be required to pass through this before the avenues to special distinction were opened. In theory perhaps this is still attempted; but in practice we seem to deviate from such a course more and more every year at Cambridge. For instance, students of classics are no longer compelled, as they formerly were, to pass a mathematical examination for their degree; and for the most part undergraduates in the colleges are excused from attendance at lectures on the subjects which they do not profess to cultivate. Even where an attempt is made to prescribe some general course the standard in each department is fixed so low as not to ensure more than the simplest rudiments of knowledge.

Much too of the prevalent culture of specialities seems to wear a sordid mercenary aspect. It is not sufficient to afford the means of study, there must be the proper share of honours and emoluments to act as a bounty or a bribe. We must not merely allow a youth to study what he pleases, but also reward him for doing so; perhaps even must appreciate him and his favourite pursuits at his own valuation.

Although I am not presumptuous enough to hold the balance between various studies, yet I shall endeavour to offer some general remarks which may assist those who are disposed to make the attempt.

As we must employ some mode of testing the diligence of teachers and the attention of pupils, it seems inevitable that there must be processes of the nature of examinations; hence it is important to pay some attention to the adaptability of subjects to the exigencies of examinations. It seems to me that the older subjects, classics and mathematics, are strongly to be recommended on the ground of the accuracy with which we can compare the relative performance of the students. In fact the definiteness of these subjects is obvious, and is commonly admitted. There is however another advantage, which I think belongs in general to these subjects, namely, that the examinations can be brought to bear upon what is really most valuable in the subjects. It is of course easy to say that the art of examination by long practice on these subjects has arrived at a degree of excellence far beyond what ought reasonably to be expected in the case of studies of quite recent popularity; but this does not seem to me to explain the matter completely. Take for instance Mathematics, and observe how real and fresh the examination papers can be made; they in fact abound in new results which are quite commensurate in importance and interest with the theorems previously established and studied. Now for a contrast take the subject of History; this may be readily admitted to be important and instructive especially for the original inquirer who has to seek for evidence, to estimate its value, and to combine it in a consistent whole. But it may be seriously doubted whether the valuable parts of the subject can be developed in our usual systems of examination. From the cases, not I admit very numerous, which have fallen under my own notice, I have formed an unfavourable judgment on this matter; it appears to me that we find in examination papers chiefly dates and striking obvious events, which form rather the skeleton of history than history itself; that the mere receptivity of the students is all that can be tested, to the exclusion of the faculties of comparison and of judgment; though these may be well developed by original researches in the subject. Thus, briefly, it seems to me that much of what constitutes the real value of mathematics can be tested by examinations, but in history there is little of this merit.

Again, take the Experimental Sciences. I am but little satisfied with what I have seen of examinations in these subjects. I have had much to do with examinations, principally but not exclusively in pure and mixed mathematics; and my experience is that nothing is so hopelessly worthless as the products of examination in experimental science. Nowhere else is the proportion of what is intelligible and true to what is absurd and false so small. Often after encountering a mass of confusion and error the disheartening conviction has been forced on the examiner that the candidates must have derived positive harm from their attempts. *Experiments* indeed strictly so called can scarcely be introduced in an examination room; in other words, the distinguishing characteristic of the subjects cannot be subjected to test. I have heard it said by an eminent professor that the intelligent use of instruments is a most essential part of natural philosophy, and that it is almost impossible to examine a large class in this matter; it would be dangerous to trust a good instrument in the hands of an average candidate. In Chemistry especially it seems to me that mere paper examination, which is all that can under ordinary circumstances be effected, is a most inadequate representation of the best parts of the subject. I may add, though it is not of much importance, that after undergoing numerous competitive examinations, and assisting in conducting many more, I have always remembered one in chemistry as the most unsatisfactory in its results.

The Natural Sciences I can speak of with only the slightest experience; but here also it seems to me that much of the real value of the subject evaporates when we bring it into the examination room. With respect to both the natural sciences and the experimental sciences it may be admitted that there is no difficulty in conducting an effective examination if the candidates are few, and the time ample; but what I wish to notice is the unsatisfactory character of the process of testing the progress of large numbers with a reasonable expenditure of examining power.

One point may be just glanced at for a moment. There must at this moment be numerous able and eminent teachers of experimental and natural science in England; but I apprehend that in extremely few cases these teachers were themselves discovered by examination tests in the subjects which they now adorn. The contrary of course holds good in mathematics and classics; here the leading authorities were almost unanimously first brought to notice by examinations in their respective pursuits; so that we have sufficient evidence that this method of transmitting instruction succeeds in these cases. But we must not assume too readily that a system which has succeeded with classics and mathematics will be equally applicable to other studies; and that distinction acquired by passing examinations will be good evidence of the existence of the capacity for teaching and investigating.

We must not lay undue stress on what may be called the examination-value of a study; those indeed who are desirous of arranging a course for self-training may neglect this consideration entirely. But those who demand an assured place for any particular study in our schemes of examination and rewards must pay attention to the point. They are bound to shew that what they consider the special benefits of the study can be well and readily tested by examinations; that is, they must shew that he who acquits himself best in an examination, conducted with the usual limits of time and expense, is really the one who knows best the valuable parts of the subject, and that he knows them well. It must be remarked that actual experience in examinations may give much information as to the educational value of certain subjects. Many persons who have been engaged in conducting the examinations for the Moral Sciences Tripos in Cambridge have found the estimate they had formed as to the merit of these studies in training the minds of the candidates much augmented.

Let me now say something as to the special advantages of mathematics. Leaving aside such points as are well known and obvious, I should like to draw attention to the inexhaustible variety of the problems and exercises which it furnishes; these may be graduated to precisely the amount of attainment which may be possessed, while yet retaining an interest and value. It seems to me that no other branch of study at all compares with mathematics in this. When we propose a deduction to a beginner we give him an exercise in many cases that would have been admired in the vigorous days of the Greek geometry. Although grammatical exercises are well suited to ensure the great benefits connected with the study of languages, yet these exercises seem to me stiff and artificial in comparison with the problems of mathematics. It is not absurd to maintain that Euclid and Apollonius would have regarded with interest many of the elegant deductions which are invented for the use of our students in geometry; but it seems scarcely conceivable that the great masters in any other line of study could condescend to give a moment's attention to the elementary books of the beginner. The possibility of the early employment of the constructive and imaginative faculties is an important gain for many students who become weary of the prolonged and unvaried exercise of mere receptive attention. In the pursuit of a new language we may secure advantages of a similar kind but probably of inferior value ; but in the early stages of most studies there seems nothing to correspond: it is scarcely conceivable that examination papers in history or the natural sciences can offer any tolerable equivalent in merit and importance to the problems of mathematics.

Another great and special excellence of mathematics is that it demands earnest voluntary exertion. It is simply impossible for a person to become a good mathematician by the happy accident of having been sent to a good school; this may give him a preparation and a start, but by his own continued efforts alone can he reach an eminent position. The rough processes by which prizes are awarded to the possessors of knowledge regard only the results offered for inspection, and overlook the finer gradations of merit which depend on the mode of acquisition. Suppose, for example, that rewards are bestowed for the cultivation of modern languages; a person who obtains the reward may have earned his distinction by his own persevering application, mainly or exclusively, but on the other hand he may owe it to the fortunate incident of residence in a foreign country, or of habitual intercourse with those who spoke the language as their vernacular. The resulting amount of knowledge is no just index of the labour and perseverance which have been expended in gaining it; the credit to be properly assigned for the accomplishment may indeed belong to the successful candidate, but it may, and perhaps more justly, be attributed entirely to his friends and relatives.

A similar consideration applies, though with diminished force, to the study of the classical languages; the foundation of knowledge in these subjects can be laid in years so early that the pupil exerts but slightly his own will; his success is a combination depending indeed partly on his own ability and application, but still more on the judgment or kind fortune which deposited him in a good school.

We repeatedly see youths enter the Universities whose position in the final classical examination is already practically assured; but distinguished success in the mathematical competition cannot be confidently expected, whatever be the ability of the candidate, unless he is willing to subject himself to steady and continued discipline. In whatever line of study distinction is sought the advantage of good teaching is great; but probably among all the pursuits of the University mathematics pre-eminently demand selfdenial, patience, and perseverance from youth, precisely at that period when they have liberty to act for themselves, and when on account of obvious temptations habits of restraint and application are peculiarly valuable.

Nor do I know any study which can compete with mathematics in general in furnishing matter for severe and continued thought. Metaphysical problems may be even more difficult; but then they are far less definite, and, as they rarely lead to any precise conclusion, we miss the power of checking our own operations, and of discovering whether we are thinking and reasoning or merely fancying and dreaming. I speak now, as on former occasions, of studies as they present themselves to minds of average power and of ordinary conditions. For persons of exceptional ability any intellectual pursuit may prove stimulating and strengthening. In other words, discoverers and original geniuses form a class apart; we may admire them, but we should not inadvertently assume that their pursuits when adopted by inferior disciples will be as vivifying as to the great masters themselves.

This is a point which has, I think, been very generally overlooked. We hear a distinguished chemist or physiologist lecture, and we are struck with the clearness of his exposition, the beauty of his language, and the fervour of his convictions; and we are sometimes inclined to suppose that if we nourish the mind of a youth on chemistry or physiology the result will be as conspicuously eminent. We may be confirmed in our anticipation, if we hear the lecturers themselves urging with enthusiasm the importance of their favourite subjects as parts of general education. But, in the first place, we may be altogether wrong in supposing that chemistry or physiology really produced the brilliant qualities which we admire—the philosophical subtlety, the poetical imagination, and the epigrammatic diction

—these may be due to far different causes, and chemistry and physiology may be only the material on which faculties are employed which would have produced a rich return on whatever field they had been exerted. And, in the second place, we are not justified in inferring that a pursuit by which an investigator himself has found excellent employment and exercise will be equally efficacious when applied as a means of instruction—that is to say, we are not sure that what constitutes the life and spirit of the original training can be preserved when it is repeated as a lesson instead of being received as an inspiration ; just as we might attempt in vain to produce a copy of the great popular orator of the day by a study of the history of the repeal of the corn laws.

The judgment of eminent masters in various departments of study with respect to the educational value of their favourite subjects is always to be received with some caution, from the fact that they rarely compute with accuracy the influence of the various forces which may have concurred in producing their own distinction. A person, for example, has in childhood commenced the study of a language, and has been compelled to master a grammar which gave him a store of facts, though exhibited in a clumsy and unscientific manner. In mature life he finds the advantage of a more elaborate arrangement and explanation of the parts of the language; and having a vivid impression of some of the least favourable characteristics of the old grammar he may strongly recommend a new and more refined treatise. But it must be almost impossible for him to estimate how much of his own

proficiency is due to the rude companion of his childhood, and to feel confident that if all he owes to that
source had been withdrawn his knowledge and his
power would remain unimpaired. His actual ability
and attainments form a complex result produced by
many causes, and it requires a profounder analysis than
a man is usually able and willing to apply to his own
case to determine with accuracy what is due to each
separate influence. The only ground then on which
the new and philosophical grammar can be safely recommended is experience, not prediction; let it be
tried and the results carefully observed.

A curious example came under my notice some
years since, which shews how hard it is for proficients
in any branch of knowledge to recal precisely the particulars of their own experience. Two mathematicians,
of good repute, both as students and as teachers, were
referring to the difficulties which perplex beginners in
the Differential Calculus; they agreed in stating that
after groping in the dark for some time light had suddenly appeared, and both regretted that in spite of
many efforts made for the purpose they could not
recollect more than this general outline.

Let me say a word on Experimental Philosophy.
This is a subject which may be considered one of the
most fashionable elements of education at the present
time; though perhaps quite recently it has rather
declined than advanced in public estimation. The
assault which has been made in our time on the
monopoly enjoyed by the older studies seems to have
been a combined movement in favour of chemistry,
natural philosophy and natural history: and I appre-

hend that natural history will in the end secure
the largest share in the conquest, if indeed it has
not already done so. In. schools it was doubtless
more interesting to many boys to assist at a lecture in chemistry or natural philosophy than to
work steadily at classics or mathematics; but chemistry and natural philosophy will in their turn be
found dull when compared with natural history, which
is associated with the love of outdoor exercise and the
desire to catch the lower animals, which are so characteristic of English youth. To have these cherished
pursuits elevated into serious duties, and dignified
with the name of studies, must have been a joyful
surprise to the generation of schoolboys who first encountered the welcome novelties.

Experimental Science, viewed in connection with
education, rejoices in a name which is unfairly expressive. A real experiment is a very valuable product
of the mind, requiring great knowledge to invent it
and great ingenuity to carry it out.

When Perrier ascended the Puy de Dôme with a
barometer in order to test the influence of change of
level in the height of the column of mercury, he performed an *experiment*, the suggestion of which was
worthy of the genius of Pascal and Descartes. But
when a modern traveller ascends Mont Blanc and
directs one of his guides to carry a barometer he
cannot be said to perform an experiment in any very
exact or very meritorious sense of the word. It is a
repetition of an observation made thousands of times
before, and we can never recover any of the interest
which belonged to the first trial, unless indeed, with-

out having ever heard of it, we succeeded in reconstructing the process for ourselves. In fact, almost always he who first plucks an experimental flower thus appropriates and destroys its fragrance and its beauty.

To take another example. We assert that if the resistance of the air be withdrawn a sovereign and a feather will fall through equal spaces in equal times. Very great credit is due to the person who first imagined the well-known experiment to illustrate this; but it is not obvious what is the special benefit now gained by seeing a lecturer repeat the process. It may be said that a boy takes more interest in the matter by seeing for himself, or by performing for himself, that is by working the handle of the air-pump: this we admit, while we continue to doubt the educational value of the transaction. The boy would also probably take much more interest in foot-ball than in Latin grammar; but the measure of his interest is not identical with that of the importance of the subjects. It may be said that the fact makes a stronger impression on the boy through the medium of his sight, that he believes it the more confidently. I say that this ought not to be the case. If he does not believe the statements of his tutor—probably a clergyman of mature knowledge, recognised ability, and blameless character—his suspicion is irrational, and manifests a want of the power of appreciating evidence, a want fatal to his success in that branch of science which he is supposed to be cultivating.

Some considerable drawback must be made from the educational value of experiments, so called, on account of their failure. Many persons must have been present at the exhibitions of skilled performers, and have witnessed an uninterrupted series of ignominious reverses; they have probably longed to imitate the cautious student who watched an eminent astronomer baffled by Foucault's experiment for proving the rotation of the earth: as the pendulum would move the wrong way the student retired, saying that he wished to retain his faith in the elements of astronomy. So great is the difficulty in persuading experiments intended to be visible to a large company to conduct themselves properly that curious charges of unfairness are in circulation, which are more or less authenticated. Thus it is said one lecturer was accustomed to shew by experiment that a body would fall down a tube in the shape of a cycloid faster than down a tube of another shape, corresponding to the same vertical height: but in order to assist nature he was wont to *grease* the ball surreptitiously which travelled on the cycloid. Again, another lecturer was accustomed to illustrate a mechanical principle known by the name of *virtual velocity:* a certain weight ought to remain immoveable, though not absolutely fixed; in this case a *nail* applied to the weight, unknown to the spectators, prevented any casualty in the experiment.

I assert then that much of what is called experimental science has no claim whatever to the title; I hope I shall not be supposed to be merely trifling with words, for I believe myself that there is an important truth involved in the remark. The function of experiment, properly so called, in the investigation of the laws and processes of nature can hardly be unduly exalted; but it may be said of the experimenter, as of

the poet, that he is born and not manufactured. The
lecture rooms of professors of experimental philosophy
must be devoted chiefly to the mechanical repetition of
familiar processes; the spectators are told what they
may expect to see, and accordingly they see it with
more or less clearness of conviction. The result of the
whole performance may be that certain facts are impressed on the belief or on the memory, but it is difficult to secure any cultivation of the power of experi-
menting, or any mode of testing the existence of such
a power. I am speaking with reference to teaching such
subjects in large classes. It may as before be readily
admitted that the force of the remarks will be much
weakened in special cases. If, for instance, two or
three pupils have the privilege of constant intercourse
with some teacher eminent for his original ·experi-
mental power, it is very natural that a training of
the highest value may thus be secured; but, setting
aside such exceptional cases, it may be held generally
that little of what is characteristically valuable in experimental philosophy is susceptible of transmission.

A remark which I have already made may deserve to
be reproduced in this connexion; for it is important
to endeavour to form an estimate of the independent
value of what is indeed experimental science, apart
from other studies. Some of the ablest teachers of
experimental science and the most strenuous advocates
of its self-sufficiency as an educational instrument, are
themselves ·persons who came to this subject after
assiduous training in other pursuits, as for instance
mathematics. I cannot help suspecting that while
they uphold the claim of experimental science as con-

2—2

stituting by itself an effectual discipline for the mind, they fail to allow in their own case for what they themselves owe to a more vigorous training. They are naturally conscious of the benefits which they have gained by their later pursuits, but they forget to enquire how much of this benefit is due to the adequate preparation ensured by their earlier studies. It is highly probable that much of the benefit may disappear when only one of the elements which formed a salutary combination in their own experience is offered singly to their pupils.

Further, not only may the subject itself lose much of its value when administered alone, but we must also remember that it may be still further deteriorated when it is taught by those who received it on an unprepared soil. There is a wide difference between experimental science as taught by a pure experimentalist, and as taught by one who has himself gained the habits of exact thought and expression in a sterner school. A distinguished chemist, only recently lost to science, once expressed in my hearing his surprise at the uniform excellence of the papers in natural philosophy sent by the pupils of a certain college, contrasted with the inferior quality of the papers in chemistry; I did not suggest the explanation though I had no doubt about it: the natural philosophy was taught by a man thoroughly trained in mathematics.

A point which I have just incidentally brought forward deserves some consideration; I mean the gradual decay in the educational value of a subject as it falls into feebler hands to administer. I do not wish to press the consideration too much, but it is obvious

that what is called experimental science in some
elementary school must be a very poor copy of what
is called by the same name in a wealthy college or
university; not only less in extent, but altogether
inferior in character. Moreover it will be just to pay
attention to this difference in the institution of competitive examinations: we must not expect boys
from the humbler classes to excel in the more expen-
sive luxuries of education.

I hope I may be excused for one remark on a tendency in education at present, more especially with
regard to the modern subjects, to render the process
interesting, as it is usually called, but amusing would
probably be the more correct word. It would be absurd
to recommend that any subject should be proposed in
a purposely repulsive form to students, especially to
youth: but, on the other hand, it seems to me a most
enervating practice to shrink from demanding even
irksome attention whenever it is necessary. The
lesson that success in any pursuit demands serious toil
must be learned eventually, and like most lessons is
learned with least pain in early years. I have seen a
sort of model lecture on a portion of natural science
which was offered to a large public school, to which I
should urge no objection if the time that it occupied
were taken from *play time*, but which seemed to me a
very unsatisfactory employment of an hour supposed
to be devoted to study. Here I may venture to draw
attention to the opinion held by the late Dr Whewell,
that natural history, chemistry, and physics should not
be made part of the business of schools, but occasionally brought under the notice of the boys by lectures:

see the *Report of the Public Schools Commission*, Vol.
II, page 43. These occasional lectures might be delivered by the eminent authorities of the period, and
thus one serious difficulty would be obviated, namely
that those who are absorbed in school-work cannot
maintain themselves at the current level of these
fluctuating subjects, and thus are in the danger of
teaching obsolete theories and demolished statements
as part of a course the essential virtue of which resides
in accuracy of information.

I have endeavoured to shew that the title Experimental Philosophy involves pretensions which cannot
be maintained so far as relates to education; I must
however admit that this is not the only case in which
an ambitious name may mislead us if we accept it
without scrutiny. For example, let us consider the
subject, which under the appellation of *Comparative
Philology* is establishing a place in our examinations.
There is a nebulous grandeur in this title which dis-
appears under careful analysis. For we soon find that
comparative philology does not even mean comparative
grammar in the full sense of the word grammar, but
merely *comparative accidence*. I am little disposed
to depreciate the claims of the classical or oriental
languages; but I attach much more importance to the
careful study of the accidence, the syntax, and the
literature of one or two than to learning the conjuga-
tion of a verb in half a dozen. I am not aware that
comparative philology has thrown light for the theo-
logian on a single text of the New Testament, or
explained to the scholar a single doubtful word in
Homer.

With respect to comparative accidence the remark is applicable which I have already made, that there may be a wide difference between the training which the first investigator derived from the pursuit, and that which it yields to the students of results already obtained. The learning and industry of Bopp, as shewn in his grammar and vocabulary, composed in the early days of Sanscrit study, deserve the highest praise; but this does not warrant us in asserting that there is a high educational value in learning portions of his works for examination purposes. There has been lately in Cambridge a dissatisfaction with the old classical examinations, and a demand for improvement. The feeling seems to have been that there was not sufficient exercise for the powers of the mind, in a course which mere schoolboys could pass through without difficulty; and accordingly some additional elements have been introduced. Grave doubts may be entertained as to the advantage which will be secured by comparative philology. As prepared for examination purposes it must apparently be merely an additional effort of memory; any thing like a problem to test the original power of the candidate seems hopeless : you cannot ask for a verb to be constructed half-way between Greek and Sanscrit because there would be no certain criterion by which to test the fiction. A student may indeed exercise himself in the way which I once heard explained by an eminent scholar; he provided himself with a few numerals in Lithuanian, I think, and then proceeded to construct the rest : here there would be a criterion, but for examination purposes the process could not be fairly estimated, because the candidate might have happened to know beforehand what the solution of the problem was.

One of the latest additions to the range of examinations in Cambridge is the construction of a Theological Tripos. This is a remarkable innovation on the custom which has so long prevailed of discouraging any special training for clergymen, at least until after they had passed through the same course as lay students. Whether the programme of the new Tripos is the most advantageous that could be constructed may well be doubted. If I may venture to offer an opinion, I regret the absence of employment for the reasoning faculties ; systematic divinity can hardly be said to be recognised, while there is an inordinate development of ecclesiastical history, and this may be safely considered as the least valuable section of history.

I have spoken of the benefit of mathematical study ; and therefore it would be unfair to omit all reference to the disadvantages.

In the first place, I think that the time which is devoted to these subjects viewed as a discipline is too long. While engaged in these pursuits a student is really occupied with a symbolical language, which is exquisitely adapted for the class of conceptions which it has to represent, but which is so very far removed from the language of common life, that unless care be taken to guard against the evil, the mathematician is in danger of finding his command over the vernacular diminished in proportion as he becomes familiar with the dialect of abstract science. It must surely be

in some degree disadvantageous to train clergymen and
barristers for several years to familiarity with a refined
and elaborate system of expression, for which they
will have little direct use in after life, and to leave
them without any cultivation of that ordinary language
which is to be the main instrument of service in their
future occupations. I estimate at a high value the
influences of mathematical study, but I am sorry to
see these benefits obtained by the sacrifice or at the
peril of any of the qualifications which are necessary
for success and for influence in practical life. There is
especially one precaution that ought to be taken. The
symbols of mathematics are so expressive that the
meaning of an investigation can be discovered by a
lenient examiner however slovenly and inaccurate the
ordinary language may be which serves to connect the
symbols. But the evil is so great which may arise
from habitual carelessness in English composition, that
examiners must be considered injudicious who do not
rigidly maintain a good standard of excellence in this
matter.

The increasing severity of our competitive examinations seems to aggravate the danger to which I refer.
Formerly all students at the University were compelled by their colleges with more or less rigour to
conform to a general course of study; ambitious mathematicians had to acquire at least a tincture of classical
and general learning; while classical students, often
sorely against their will, were compelled at Cambridge
to undergo a mathematical training. Much of this
system has been recently relaxed or dissolved. Many
eminent scholars now regret the exemption of the

classical students from nearly all their mathematical
training; and it is I believe a still more serious evil
if students intent mainly on mathematics are allowed
to remain without a due counterpoise of other studies.
I do not suppose that the candidates who attain to the
highest places in the Mathematical Tripos are deficient
in knowledge and interest in other subjects; but I fear
that omitting these more distinguished men, the remainder frequently betray a rude ignorance in much
that is essential to a liberal education.

In our University mathematical training, there is
I think, what may be called a wearisome and unprofit-
able monotony; I speak of course with respect to the
disciplinary character of the process. For example : a
person gains a certain knowledge of a new subject, like
the Differential Calculus; the fresh conceptions which
this involves are important and instructive. But after
gaining these conceptions, months may be spent in
incessant practice in deductions and problems, so as to
leave no weak spot which an examiner's lance could
penetrate. Of course if the object is to produce a
mathematical professor this elaborate drill may be
accepted, though perhaps even then not absolutely
necessary. But considered as a part of general education, although the minute accuracy which it tends
to produce may be admired, yet it may well be
doubted if the profit is commensurate with the expenditure of time and labour. The process seems a
modern innovation. In the study of mathematics
formerly, as a discipline, a general knowledge of the
principles was all that was required; now we insist
on a minute investigation of every incidental part of

the subject. Exceptions and isolated difficulties seem to receive undue attention, on account of their utility for the examiner's purpose.

The great progress which Mathematical science has made in late years, while increasing largely its power, considered as an instrument for the original investigator, has not necessarily promoted its educational value for ordinary students. I remember to have heard from the late Professor Boole, an opinion which I had also formed myself, that the increase in the resources of notation tended to diminish the importance of mathematics as a discipline. If we take for example the modern methods of abridged notation in algebraical geometry, while we must admire the genius which has created and developed such a remarkable system of investigation, yet we must see that when it is cultivated for examination purposes there is the great danger that the symbols may be used as substitutes for thought rather than as aids to thought.

It may perhaps sound paradoxical to complain of the merits of text-books, but yet it may be doubted whether by improving the accuracy and extending the range of our explanatory treatises, we increase the value of Mathematics as a discipline. The high road of mathematics is now so well laid out and preserved as seriously to impair the advantages which might arise from the exercise of individual circumspection to prevent wandering. While I was myself constantly engaged in the teaching of mathematics, it often occurred to me that the peculiar benefits of the study were experienced in a very high degree in the early part of the course; then during the long period which the student

occupied in passing through subject after subject under
the influence of the trustworthy text-books, the advantage seemed by no means proportional to the time
and the labour spent in the pursuit. The conspicuous
merit of the subject seemed to reappear when the
students arrived at the higher parts of the course
where there remained serious difficulties which had not
been explained at all, or of which the explanations did
not appear in the accessible elementary treatises.

I can only touch on the Natural Sciences; my
experience does not justify me in offering an opinion
on more than one point, and that is the claim which is
often put forward, that the study of these sciences is
eminently and especially salutary as a means of deve-
loping the powers of observation. I cannot admit
the validity of this claim. The study of any subject
tends to make men observant of the special matter of
that subject; the study of botany doubtless trains the
habit of observing botanical phenomena; the study
of chemistry doubtless trains the habit of observing
chemical phenomena. But I have never noticed that
the devotion to any specific branch of natural history
or natural philosophy has any potent influence in rendering the student specially alive to phenomena unconnected with the specific pursuit: I could give some
striking examples to the contrary.

To pass for a moment to something of a kindred
character, I have occasionally heard a similar claim
advanced as to the cultivation of the powers of observation for the occupation of an artist; I do not think
that the claim can be substantiated. Thus much I
may say; in my experience with pupils I learned to

look with apprehension on any exhibition of artistic
skill among students of mathematics: for I am sure
that it was not a fancy but an actual fact that such
a power was in many cases an obstacle to success.
In a subject like elementary geometry, where good
diagrams might be executed for elementary problems,
those who could draw well seemed occasionally to
have an advantage over those who could not. But
in such a subject as solid geometry, where the diagrams are more difficult, and sometimes scarcely prac-
ticable, it seemed to me that artistic skill might be
an actual impediment: it too often happened that what
could not be drawn could not be imagined, and the
mind long accustomed to work with the aid of the
fingers could not act independently. Certainly there
are exceptions; I remember two very distinguished
pupils who drew well, and possessed the powers of
apprehension and of reasoning in the highest excellence: but the main stream of my experience ran in
the contrary direction.

I have not space to discuss the matter fully, but
I am persuaded that the *science of observation* is far
from maturity. The notion seems to me dangerously
prevalent that seeing and hearing are operations of the
body, namely of the eye and ear respectively, instead
of mental processes conducted through the instrumen-
tality of these organs. Wellington once in India arrived at a troublesome river which he had apparently
no means of crossing; but a glance of his eye shewed
him at a certain part of the stream two villages opposite each other on the two banks; his mind assured
him that in all probability there must be a ford con-

necting the villages, and this proved to be the case.
I may be thought rash, but I cannot help recording
the opinion that the tendency of some of the fashionable studies of the day is to lead men to see the
villages with the eye of the body, and to count the
number of huts in each, but to overlook the ford
accessible to the mental vision.

A consideration which seems to me almost entirely
neglected is that of the relative importance of studies.
A certain subject may be recommended as valuable,
but it by no means follows that it is the duty or
even the privilege of a particular person to pursue
it : he should ask if this is the study which it is most
suitable or most obligatory for him to undertake. It
is not uncommon to find, for example, that while all
persons are urged to engage in certain researches the
clergy are especially invited to pursue them : thus
natural and experimental philosophy are sometimes
pressed on their attention. But surely the question
is not what branch of study will be useful for clergymen, but what will be most useful; or rather what
is most stringently imperative upon them. I can
hardly conceive that any person will seriously deny
that Latin and Greek are essential ; and that Hebrew,
Theology, Mental and Moral Philosophy, and Ecclesiastical History, all have claims which it may be
difficult to adjust accurately, but which seem to stand
before the natural and experimental sciences. For in
the present day the clergy are not expected to be
authorities on these extra-professional subjects; but
we do look to them for biblical criticism, theology,
and moral philosophy. I say nothing against the

employment of the time in any innocent relaxation; but it does appear to me that if those who undertake the responsibility of the Christian ministry arrange their studies in the order of obligation, then few besides those of great ability and abundant leisure will arrive at the point when it is incumbent on them to pursue with seriousness such subjects as physiology or galvanism.

But it is time to conclude. As a general principle it may be said that the older practice in education was to aim at the discipline of the mind, and that the modern seeks to store with information; then naturally the older practice was to constrain youth to pass through certain compulsory courses, while the modern leaves abundant liberty of selection. It is curious that in America, which might be supposed to adopt the modern practice without hesitation, there are symptoms of a reaction of opinion in favour of the older course: I will quote a few words from the Report on Education in the United States and Canada by the present Bishop of Manchester, page 178:

"I found a widely spread fear, in many directions, of the encroachments of the physical sciences on the general domain of education, as though they were trying to occupy the whole ground. We have already seen the fate of the Classics: and even the Mathematics, I was told, can hardly maintain their position even in the Universities of Yale and Harvard. They get 'crowded out' by other studies of more 'immediate practical utility.'"

COMPETITIVE EXAMINATIONS.

OURS is an age of examinations; and the University of Cambridge may claim the merit of originating this characteristic of the period. When we hear, as we often do, that the Universities are effete bodies which have lost their influence on the national character, we may point with real or affected triumph to the spread of Examinations as a decisive proof that the humiliating assertion is not absolutely true. Although there must have been in schools and elsewhere processes resembling examinations before those of Cambridge had become widely famous; yet there can be little chance of error in regarding our Mathematical Tripos as the model for rigour, justice and importance, of a long succession of institutions of a similar kind which have since been constructed.

Many may hope, and perhaps some few believe, that we are not destined to be always fettered in teaching and in study by the pressure of impending examinations; that hereafter the ways of learning may be more pleasant and her paths more peaceful than they are now, amidst the feverish excitement of our unceasing competitive strifes; but there seems at present little prospect of early improvement. New examinations are continually announced; but as far as I

know there is no obituary record concerning the extinction of any which have been illustrious in the past.
When any examination is reconstituted the changes
made are nearly invariably in the direction of enlarged
extent and more stringent rigour. We are now apparently on the point of inaugurating, as the newspapers
say, a systematic examination of the large public
schools under the supervision of the University. Moreover, after contriving examinations in countless forms
and circumstances for youths and men, a new field has
been opened for the display of like ingenuity by extending the benefits of these disciplinary arrangements to
the other sex ; and already three schemes are in operation adjusted to different ages. However, one eminent
scholar among us encourages us with the prophecy,
that in about twenty years examinations will have
ceased in Cambridge ; he holds that, as the disease
attacked us first, and assumed here its most virulent
type, we may hope to be the first to recover.

But perhaps we must be prepared to allow that
examinations are to some extent *necessary.* Among
teachers there will be always a great diversity of
attainments and of power, different standards of excellence and degrees of energy; and hence it may be
difficult to distinguish sufficiently between zeal and
indolence, between ability and incapacity, except by
the examination of the pupils. Moreover teachers,
especially when young and without experience, may
feel anxious to see some test of the value of their
methods such as the examination of their pupils furnishes.

Still it might be contended that all the useful

effects of examinations could be secured without conducting them on such an elaborate scale as at present; by making them rather of a qualifying than of a competitive character. Thus a school or a college might be content with its own processes, conducted by its own staff or by its own chosen examiners, and might leave unnoticed the numerous competitive tests which solicit candidates on all sides. Perhaps, with teachers of eminent ability and influential character, such an arrangement might succeed; they would rely on their reputation and their genius to make their courses of instruction attractive without any direct concession to the general demand for artificial stimulants;· certainly one such teacher venerated by his pupils, presents himself to my memory while I write. I fear, however, that it may be said of him as of the great philanthropist, that "he trod an open but unfrequented path to immortality." Few are found to imitate his example; and we must resign ourselves to the fact that education is for the most part directed to training pupils for examination.

Notwithstanding however the large development of examinations in modern times it does not appear that this method of testing ability and attainments is accepted without hesitation. On the contrary, complaints are loud and numerous, not so much against examinations themselves as against certain real or supposed faults in the mode of conducting them. It is customary to supply some opprobrious epithet to any real or imaginary abuse as a preliminary to a serious attack. The received word in the present case is *cramming*, which has the great advantage of sounding very unpleasantly, and yet being destitute of any fixed definite meaning, as indeed might be expected from its meta-phorical nature. It has I think been a grave error in discussions on examinations, instead of clearly stating what may be held to be their advantages or disad-vantages, to diverge into abuse of an ill-defined phantom called *cram.*

It may perhaps be conjectured that one fault attach-ing to examinations against which this vague epithet is levelled, consists in the tendency they have to over cultivation and over appreciation of the *memory.* This however can hardly be helped, owing to the essential character of an examination. Suppose, for example, that the subject of examination is a *language;* it would seem from the nature of the case that the memory must be the principal faculty that is tested. To know a language means chiefly to know the grammar and the dictionary of that language ; so that the more powerful the memory is, the more easily is the task of learning discharged, and the greater the success attained in any conceivable method of trial and investigation. Even in mathematics, where the memory might at first be supposed to play a subordinate part, we shall find by experience that similar conclusions hold. Whatever may be the inventive power and the genius of a candi-date, it is a simple fact that one who relies mainly on his own resources cannot produce within the limits of time allowed for an examination, solutions which shall rival in accuracy and beauty those which a well stored memory can furnish. It might be objected that in a mathematical examination, by excluding all propositions worked out in the books, and giving only examples

3—2

and problems, a test might be devised which would appeal almost exclusively to the reasoning faculty. But there are two objections to this course. In the first place such a kind of examination would be in general too difficult. It would not adequately measure the industry and the application of those who are able to follow a mathematical argument and derive great benefit from the habit of close attention which is thus strengthened, but have little original power. On the other hand, the attempt to place the student with a bad and ill-trained memory more nearly on a level with a better equipped competitor would fail; for practically the solution of problems, at least within reasonable limits of time, cannot be undertaken with any prospect of success unless a large store of formulæ and types of investigation can be readily and accurately recalled.

Nor can it be considered an evil in itself that the memory should be mainly exercised in examinations. In teaching children this must be the faculty which has first to be cultivated; and it is, I think, only when we attempt to extract too much by our examinations, to make them the serious occupation of men instead of the initiatory discipline of youth, that we are open to the charge of unduly exalting the memory.

But to come to particular cases. I have heard examiners in Latin and Greek sometimes complain that candidates have learned a translation by heart, and written it out; when it appeared from the answers to grammatical questions that they were unable to render the Latin and Greek, word for word, into

English. Such cases however are not very numerous ; and it would be possible to guard against them if necessary. It might be made compulsory to write out the original and the translation word for word together. Or it might be appointed that the translation should not count at all unless certain grammatical questions, and certain easy sentences taken from a book not previously fixed, should be fairly managed. I believe however that if proper discretion is allowed to examiners, little danger will exist of such an evil as I have here noticed ; but it must be confessed that examiners are frequently hampered by the restraints of the regulations under which they act. This is more especially the case with modern schemes and boards of examination ; the official programme is sometimes drawn up, and the system administered by men who, however highly distinguished, are themselves practically without any experience in teaching or examining.

Let us, however, consider the evil which has been brought forward in connexion with mathematical examinations. A proposition is set which a candidate writes out correctly ; nevertheless by comparing the candidate's other papers, it may be highly probable, or even almost certain, that he wrote it out from memory without understanding it. How is such a case to be treated ? Perhaps those who give any definite meaning to the word *cramming* would apply it here, where the candidate has drawn from his memory alone what his reason ought to have shaped and controlled.

I am of opinion that the frequency of such cases

has been exaggerated. One more usually hears such things from the candidate than from the examiner; the former may flatter himself that his ignorance was undetected, when the latter could tell a different tale. Even a powerful memory is apt to prove treacherous during the excitement of an examination, when employed without the aid of the reason on difficult and unfamiliar matter. Stories are in circulation which may well shake the firmest faith in the power of the accurate reproduction of what the mind has never mastered : one instance was handed down by tradition, in which a long piece of astronomy was learned by heart and written out accurately according to the candidate's belief, but an extraordinary displacement of a stop revealed the secret to the examiner's suspicious eye.

If such attempts to gain credit for knowledge not actually acquired were numerous, it would be necessary and possible to guard against them by due regulations. Of course proper notice would have to be given if the rules of estimating the value of papers had to be rendered in any manner more stringent. It is recorded that many years since the mathematical examiners acted for once on the rule of giving no marks whatever for the propositions set unless the candidate also solved the example or deduction which is frequently attached as a *rider* to a proposition. Such a rule might be advantageous, provided due notice had been previously given that it would be introduced ; but the examiners who enforced it without any preparatory warning are justly held to have behaved with great indiscretion and harshness.

While I hope and believe that there are really few cases in which a candidate would deliberately attempt to commit to memory an investigation quite beyond the range of his understanding, yet I think it possible that there may not unfrequently be cases in which a proposition is partially understood and the memory may be required to supply the infirmity of the reason. In such cases we may charitably trust that further application would conquer the remaining difficulty, and may lean to the side of liberality rather than of severity in estimating the merits of the candidate. On the whole, I suppose that the usual course is to give a candidate full marks for what he has done correctly, even though portions of his work should be much above the level of his average performances ; nor do I think that any very appreciable evil is thus produced.

We cannot, however, fail to observe that attempts are occasionally made to bring into action some check to control or correct the mere numerical return of marks, especially when various subjects are combined in an examination so as to form an aggregate of merit.

One contrivance which has been adopted is that of striking off a certain number of marks from those obtained in any subject, so as to prevent a candidate from accumulating a large total by slender proficiency in numerous subjects. The design probably is to discourage smatterers ; and the belief probably is that the elements of a subject are easy and therefore should not be liberally rewarded. The creed seems to me unsound, and the practice which is founded on it unwise. An old proverb says that the first step is the great difficulty; and my own experience and observation suggest to me that the commencement of a new study is the stage at which the greatest resolution is required, and liberal encouragement most useful. An objection to smattering is, I presume, not really an objection to slight knowledge as such, or in comparison with ignorance, but rather to the attempt to obtain from such slight knowledge the credit due only to an ample store; such an attempt, however, before a competent board of examiners, as well as before the large tribunal of the world, is usually made in vain.

If, however, the principle really at the base of such a rule for discouraging fragments of knowledge is deliberate preference of extensive attainments in one subject rather than of moderate attainments in a variety of subjects, then I apprehend the practice is not carried far enough. Not only should all the marks be rejected which fall below a prescribed minimum for each subject, but also it should be imperative for a candidate to reach in some one subject a tolerably high standard. I should however, for my own part, be disposed to lay down no such rules; but simply evaluate as well as possible any knowledge, narrow or wide, which might be exhibited on the subjects of the examination. I regard all knowledge as valuable, and I regret to see a person discouraged from commencing any study because his engagements and his opportunities may not allow him to become profound and famous in it.

The most favourite prescription, however, for the supposed defects of our paper examinations is the introduction of *vivâ voce* examinations. It seems to me that on this matter there has been much extravagant expectation, and many unreasonable suggestions; and often a fatal confusion between competitive examinations and mere pass examinations.

Let us suppose that we are dealing simply with a pass examination. This will be necessarily of an elementary character: for example, we may have to ascertain whether the candidate knows the elements of Latin, or whether he understands the first three books of Euclid. Then we may admit that the process of a *vivâ voce* examination is easy, short, and satisfactory. In many cases a candidate will clearly shew in a few minutes that he has acquired the prescribed minimum of knowledge, or of reasoning power; in not a few cases he will as quickly and as certainly expose his intolerable ignorance or stupidity. Only a small minority of the cases will be of that uncertain character as to demand the examiner's prolonged attention in order to arrive at a just decision.

But in a competitive examination the circumstances are very different. Here every question must be carefully marked, and the examiner must be watchful to make his questions of the same order of difficulty for all the candidates. The practical obstacles are very serious. If the examination is short, the candidate has scarcely time to gain confidence and self-possession; if the examination is long, the labour becomes so oppressive that the expenses of the examination are seriously increased in order to recompense the services of competent examiners. Doubtless by the temptation of adequate salaries, we may secure eminent men for this work; but whether such an outlay would be a judicious employment of funds may well be questioned. It is easy to refine and elaborate our examination machinery; but the results will scarcely repay the expenditure of money, time and ability. We cannot by our examinations *create* learning or genius; it is uncertain whether we can infallibly *discover* them; what we detect is simply the examination-passing-power of the candidates, and this can be adequately appreciated by simpler and less costly processes.

Of course there are cases in which a *vivâ voce* examination may be recommended or justified by peculiar circumstances. The *vivâ voce* examination may in fact, though not in name, be a personal inspection of the candidates with the view of identifying them, or of detecting any objectionable peculiarities of manner, appearance or language. Again, there may be in a college a sufficient staff of residents competent and willing to conduct the operations; and then these obvious resources may be employed, just as we may avail ourselves of a spontaneous supply of water-power when it would be extravagantly unremunerative to employ a steam-engine.

Supposing however that a competitive examination is to be conducted, in which a *vivâ voce* element is to be introduced, there is a serious difficulty which presents itself at the beginning. Of course the whole time available is so arranged and subdivided that for each candidate only a certain definite portion can be assigned. An examiner finds, we will suppose, that he can on the average propose thirty questions to each candidate in the time allowed. It is essential that the

examiner should be just, that is uniformly stringent or
uniformly lenient. Now is he to make it his object to
find out the knowledge or the ignorance of the candidate? Is he to endeavour to give as many marks as
possible or as few? The answer which the candidate
returns to the first question proposed to him may not
unfrequently throw such light on the state of his mind
as to shew the examiner that by pursuing one path he
will be able to award marks liberally, and by pursuing
another he will only record a blank. If the examiner
is confident that his duty is to unmask ignorance, or
that it is to reveal knowledge, and if he can rely on
himself to act unflinchingly on his convictions, his course
is clear. But if he is undecided as to the theory on
which he ought to proceed, or fluctuating in practice,
he may be extremely perplexed as to what he ought to
do at various critical points of his interview with the
candidate. Perhaps in many cases the examiner will
come to the conclusion that he must go straight through
the course of questions which he had antecedently fixed
in his mind as constituting a fair allotment for the
individual to be subjected to his scrutiny.

The merit and importance of *vivâ voce* examinations
have been however so strongly urged by various eminent
persons in the University of Cambridge, that I feel
bound to say a few more words on the subject. I will
acknowledge then that if only two or three candidates
have to be examined, and we have the command of
unlimited time and of adequate examining force, then
whatever may be the subject of examination, the *vivâ
voce* method may be not only allowed but strongly
recommended. We may ascertain with respect to each

candidate both what he knows and what he does not know, and whether he shews evidence of independent power.

But when larger numbers have to be handled, the possibility of using a *vivâ voce* element with advantage, may turn very much on the nature of the subject of examination. Suppose this subject to be a language ; say Latin or Greek. The book or books for consideration supply an inexhaustible store of passages for translation, while almost each sentence suggests appropriate grammatical and other questions; and these questions are such as may be answered off-hand, for they are of necessity mainly addressed to the memory. The examiner in fact has an ample store of materials naturally collected exactly suitable to his purpose.

But with mathematical subjects the case is very different. We cannot expect a candidate to repeat a demonstration fluently by heart, except it be in a very elementary subject, like Euclid, where the diagram is a perpetual reminder of the stage at which the argument has arrived. The stock of suitable questions is very small; for if they are to correspond to the best part of mathematical science they must be addressed to the reason mainly, and not to the memory : and it is not easy to find a large number of points which a candidate can be fairly expected to think out for himself in an examination room without any mechanical aid. As a matter of experience we find the candidates repeatedly assuring the examiners that with the aid of pen and paper the question could be readily solved; of course if such a concession is made the so called *vivâ voce* examination loses very much of the advantage which on the ground of variety and rapidity may be challenged for it. In fact what really results is a paper examination, with the drawback however that as the same questions may not have been given to all the candidates the appreciation of relative merit becomes harder and less trustworthy.

I have never seen any pretence at meeting the practical difficulties which would occur if *vivâ voce* examinations in the higher parts of mathematics are to be introduced into our University system. The examination would I presume be conducted in public; and then I cannot imagine how any adequate stock of questions suitable to the purpose can be provided. It seems to me that the examiner would necessarily exhaust his resources in dealing with the first two or three candidates; afterwards he could only repeat what he had already divulged, and for which accordingly the candidates would be prepared. Even if the examination professes to be private it will still be impossible to prevent a candidate who has made the voyage from communicating his experience to a friend who has not yet started; thus furnishing him in effect with a chart on which are marked all the dangerous rocks.

I do not lay stress on details, otherwise it would I believe be easy to demonstrate the impossibility of any thing like a real *vivâ voce* examination in the more abstruse parts of mathematics. Nor need I do more than allude to the difficulty of obtaining efficient examiners, the labour and responsibility imposed on them being much greater than under the existing system. It is obvious that a man who selects his own questions and then examines at his leisure the answers submitted to him, guided by his books and assisted by the mutual comparison of the papers, may acquit himself with perfect credit, while yet he might shrink from engaging as it were in single combat with an able candidate in a high state of preparation.

A very eminent private tutor in Cambridge suggested a variety of the *vivâ voce* examinations, which may be briefly noticed. He proposed that for the higher and more important subjects there should be, as at present, printed questions; but that after the answers had been written, each candidate should be examined *vivâ voce* on his own papers. The design doubtless would be to ascertain if the candidate really understood what he had written, or merely reproduced it from memory. Still, the practical difficulties of which I have already spoken would exist with little alleviation. Moreover a candidate, directly after he had written his answers, would seek the assistance of his friends and tutors, and would fortify himself as to all the points which were likely to come under discussion; so that he might completely baffle the examiner's attempts to convict him of ignorance.

The late Mr Hopkins, for many years the most celebrated private tutor in Cambridge, was a strong advocate for the introduction of a *vivâ voce* examination. He used to say that there were cases in which, from his knowledge of his pupils, he could not acquiesce in the correctness of the relative positions assigned to them by the examiners; and he felt confident that in these cases a *vivâ voce* examination would have led to the proper arrangement. But with the greatest possible respect for my honoured master and friend, I was, and am, unable to agree with his opinion. In the first place, as I have already urged, the practical difficulties which beset us in endeavouring to constitute a *vivâ voce* examination which shall be really influential in deciding the places of the candidates are enormous; indeed, I think them insuperable. In the second place, we must carefully distinguish between a *vivâ voce* examination when first started, and when it has become a long established institution. Speaking generally, I should maintain that, as candidates now carefully prepare for a paper examination, so they would carefully prepare for a *vivâ voce* examination, as soon as its nature and its influence on academical distinction had become well settled and understood. Then the same fortunate combination of qualities which obtains success under one system would almost universally obtain it under the other.

Although I fear that, whatever may be our scheme of examination, it is impossible to prevent training from encroaching on genius, yet it may be possible to make such a modification of our system as to lead to more varied and more valuable training. I need scarcely say that any such modification should be introduced with due consideration and after ample notice. I have already adverted to the impropriety of arbitrary revolutions in the system of examinations at the caprice of the current examiners.

There are two suggestions as to examinations which I have frequently offered in conversations and in discussions, and which have been generally well received. One of these is what may be called the system of *negative* marks. Our actual method is to give a candidate marks for all that he works correctly, and to leave his errors unnoticed. I think it might be reasonable and desirable to give marks for correct work, and to *subtract marks* for errors. Suppose that one candidate has solved twenty questions all correctly; and suppose that another has also solved twenty questions all correctly, and has attempted four more and failed completely in them; then, assuming that the questions are on an average of equal value, the two candidates would be pronounced equal on our actual method. Yet it may happen that the four failures betray such ignorance and incapacity as to demand some more decisive condemnation than simple want of notice. I am not referring to mere inaccuracies of numerical calculation or temporary lapses; these are always treated leniently by examiners. I have in view deliberate, gross blunders, which the candidate has put down without any hesitation, and which, if he were cross-examined, he would maintain as firmly as any other part of his work. In the actual business of life, for which our examinations ought to form some kind of preparatory discipline and training, decisive errors and failures are not estimated as simple blanks; they justly tell heavily against their author. I conclude that when we are estimating the value of a candidate's attainments, we ought to appreciate the evidence which he furnishes by the rule which we should invariably apply to every practical matter; namely, we should count in his favour all that exhibits his knowledge, and count against him all that reveals ignorance and incapacity. My own experience of examinations leads me to the conviction that, when the results have appeared to me open to objection, the fault has arisen from the system being so constructed as to favour speed with inaccuracy at the expense of deliberate precision and certainty.

Although I venture to consider the system of *negative marks* as thus possessing obvious recommendations, yet I will admit that the advantage which it offers might perhaps be secured indirectly in another way, namely by confining our examination papers within such reasonable limits of length that a person could, if adequately prepared, solve all the questions in the prescribed time. At present, as Dr Whewell once observed to me, our candidates are tempted to scribble in tempestuous haste, and send to the examiners the result without any revision. I should like to see the papers so short that mere rapidity of handwriting could exert no influence, and the candidate would either solve every question or, by his omission, confess his inability. At present, such a phenomenon as the following is not impossible in an examination room; A and B sit down to a paper containing twenty problems; A, swift and ready, may solve ten in the prescribed time, while B, more deliberate, may solve eight: but on the other hand, if the time were extended, A might be unable to add to his number, while B might be competent to solve all. As long as we make our papers so extensive as to require at least double the time which is nominally assigned to them, so long do we encourage quickness rather than certainty; nay so long do we run the risk of elevating rapid penmanship into competition with genius and learning.

I pass to my second suggestion; and I restrict myself to these two, though conjectural emendations in the schemes of examinations are as facile and as seductive as in the range of verbal criticism.

It may be, I think, justly charged upon our examinations that the memory is over cultivated and rewarded. As I have already said, examinations in some subjects, as in languages, for example, must necessarily be almost exclusively tests of the memory; but what we may regret to see is, that in examinations in subjects with which the reasoning power is supposed to be mainly concerned, the memory should be severely taxed. Owing to the great extension of mathematics in recent times, we have now special investigations which apply to whole classes of problems, starting the enquirer, as it were, on the track required for the solution, and executing much of the preliminary work. Thus, when a problem is proposed, a student, if he attempts to begin with some general formula, has to go through a large amount of reduction and transformation before he can arrive at the particular expressions which are the most suitable, or it may be which are alone suitable, for the process which he is required to perform. Another student, however, who can draw from his memory the particular expressions which are adapted to his purpose, has already half accomplished his task before his competitor has commenced the essential part of the solution. A good example is furnished by the subject of analytical Dynamics; the fundamental formulæ may be modified in many ways, by adopting various systems of fixed or moving axes, and each modification will be peculiarly suitable for a corresponding class of problems. Now, a mathematician of high power would be able, with adequate time, to deduce from the fundamental formulæ the precise modification which the occasion may require ; but this will not be sufficient for the purposes of a successful examination : he must be able to quote instantaneously instead of merely deducing accurately. Yet it must not be supposed that the solution of a problem is a mechanical process, requiring merely the use of a well furnished memory ; for there is still room for a large amount of judgment in selecting the materials treasured up, and for skill in the combination of them, but an ample and accessible supply of the necessary materials is indispensable.

In all the higher departments of mathematics where the investigations are long and difficult, unless large parts of them are fixed in the memory, they cannot be reproduced within the slender limits of time which the exigencies of an examination impose. The precise combination of mathematical facts required at each stage of the operation may have been discovered by the ingenuity of many investigators, protracted over many years, and involving often the trial and rejection of various tempting but inadequate processes ; and it would be presumptuous for any single person to hope to rival the mature efforts of the great masters of science. Moreover a slight numerical inaccuracy at one point of a long mathematical investigation will not unfrequently completely vitiate all that follows ; so that unless there is the check which is furnished by the recollection of what the results ought to be at the successive stages, there is considerable risk of arriving after much time and labour at hopeless confusion. On account of their length and intricacy many valuable and important propositions cannot be set in the examinations with any reasonable prospect of getting them written out; and hence the custom has arisen of reading only selected portions of a subject instead of the whole, the selection being made by the tutor. Thus we are in danger of over-estimating the knowledge of our students; we see that it is exact over a certain range, and we forget that the range is narrow.

I would suggest that a part or the whole of the examination in the higher branches of mathematics should be conducted with the aid of assigned books. For instance, if the subject is the Figure of the Earth, the candidates might be allowed to take into the room the second volume of the *Mécanique Céleste*, and be examined in it. The examination would then involve the explanation of any passages in the book, together with inferences and extensions to be deduced from it. Still I must confess that the difficulty might occur here which I have already noticed, namely, the want of sufficient variety: we might expect to find in the course of one or two years all the natural questions that could be set, discovered and used; the exhausted examiners would try in vain for novelties to adorn their papers, and the students would store their memories with all which the past had furnished in order to prepare for the future. It has been suggested that examiners have a faculty directly contrary to that which Johnson ascribed to Goldsmith; instead of adorning, they seem to spoil what they touch : and however cunningly we may devise our schemes for discovering native talent we shall in the main give our rewards to assiduous culture, honouring the teacher rather than the pupil.

Nothing that has been said must be taken to imply any depreciation of the memory, or any desire to check the cultivation of it. But there may be a tendency to suppose that which we see in one department of knowledge to be readily applicable to another. By all means let the memory of the young be well stored with the choicest passages in prose and poetry which the languages they study can supply. On the one hand the labour of acquisition is not too difficult; and on the other hand the beauty of form constitutes a large part of the value of the combination of thought and expression which is urged on the attention of the learner. But as to mathematical investigations, on the one hand the difficulty of fixing them in the memory is very great, and on the other hand the *form* is of little value compared with the reasoning which it involves.

The difficulty which the daily increase of the matter in scientific subjects causes in our examination schemes seems to be very serious. In mathematics we have perpetual additions both to our elementary and to our higher works. We may hope that owing to enlarged knowledge many of the isolated processes and investigations will hereafter be reduced under general theorems; and thus our science will become at once more extensive in range and more compendious in expression; but there seems at present little of such tendency. So far as I may express any opinion on the natural and experimental sciences, the facts seem to be ever augmenting, and consequently also the strain which must be exerted on the memory in order to meet the possible

demands of examiners. Some illustration of the nature
of the case may be borrowed from the game of chess;
I am told that every possible variety of the first few
moves must be committed to memory to form, as it
were, the book-work of the subject: and it is conceivable that this task may be always· augmenting until
it demands the energy of a whole life.

We have been led again to what I have already
pointed out as a real and I fear insuperable difficulty
with respect to examinations; namely, that they tend
to make cultivation superior to genius. It seems to me
that this, in conjunction with the recent changes in the
Universities, must operate seriously to the disadvantage of the poorer classes. By our present arrangements
we have numerous minor scholarships and exhibitions,
which are awarded by competition at the commencement of the University course. It is obvious that these
prizes cannot be gained by mere ability; the candidates
must have had long and careful preparation at the
hands of able teachers, themselves stimulated by the
credit and advantage which will accrue to them from the
distinctions acquired by their pupils. Those who are
successful in these preliminary contests fall under the notice and obtain the encouragement of the college tutors;
and owing to their early promise, and to the acquisition
of the necessary means, they can secure the assistance of
the best private tutors in the place; and it need scarcely
be said that this assistance must be costly. The result
is, that however great may be the natural power of a
candidate, unless he has had an excellent antecedent
training, he cannot in general press to the front during
the time allowed for the academic race. I look on the

change which has been thus produced as most disastrous. I fear it would not be possible now to have a repetition of the incidents with which former generations
were familiar, where a poor student entering the University with great ability though with but little cultivation, ultimately gained the highest honours of the place.
According to our present system, it would appear that
except by unusual accident, we must draw all our
recruits for the higher intellectual pursuits of the
country from the upper and middle classes who are in
easy circumstances ; large as the supply may thus
appear to be, it falls far short of what we might hope
to gain if the avenues to academical honours were
practically open to the entire population. Let us hope
however that by the establishment of schools of various
grades throughout the country it will ultimately become easy to draw to the University all the rising
talent of the country.

Not unfrequently attempts have been suggested,
rather than made, with the view of diminishing the
amount of training through which our students pass
before they present themselves for examination. It
has been even proposed that private tuition should be
expressly prohibited. I could not recommend such a
course even if I thought private tuition as great an
evil as they must do who would try to suppress it by
positive enactment. In the first place it would be
impossible to enforce such a law. Even assuming for a
moment that something could be done to ensure obedi-
ence at the University itself, it is manifest that during
the vacations, which are much longer than the necessary terms of residence, no control could be exerted

over the students. In the second place, an undergraduate who had an older friend or relative in the University, though not formally receiving private tuition, must obtain very great benefit from the intercourse which would naturally subsist between himself and his senior. Thus in fact by private tuition a great advantage is secured to wealth over poverty; if private tuition were prohibited, this specific inequality might be removed, but there would arise instead the evils, not less serious, which personal friendship or family connexion would produce.

There is one danger from which we ought to protect our examinations, and that is the undue prevalence of a solitary type of examiners. The danger is not altogether visionary; for it has been experienced in the two great departments of study which are most cultivated in the University. Hence has arisen a complaint that besides the four recognised ancient dialects of Greek, a student must render himself familiar with a fifth, which is modern and peculiar to a famous school, in order to guarantee himself against his probable examiners. In the mathematical examinations some variety is ensured by not leaving a monopoly to any one College, and by not employing the same examiner too frequently; but still there is nothing to prevent us from having a body of examiners consisting principally, or even entirely, of pupils of the same teacher. If the examiners were men of independent power, and engaged in the prosecution of their mathematical studies, we may admit that little harm could arise; the peculiarities of early instruction would have disappeared under the influence of subsequent original study and research.

But if these conditions do not hold ; if the examiner has only acquiesced in what his teacher put before him, and for want of inclination or of leisure has not advanced himself beyond the point to which he had been conducted, we are liable to have in his questions only a reproduction of the favourite points and peculiarities of his master ; and thus an undue advantage is gained by those who have themselves issued from the fortunate school. I am decidedly of opinion that the evil of which I have spoken has really existed in comparatively recent times.

I pass, by a natural transition, to record my opinion on a very important point,—as it would not be honest to conceal the strong conviction which I feel. I hold that the greatest strictness ought to be maintained in excluding every person from examining in a competitive examination those who have been his own pupils. I am astonished to see how completely the necessity and the reason for such a regulation are overlooked or denied. It is commonly said that an examiner will be scrupulously just in holding the balance between those whom he examines, whether his own pupils or not. I admit this unreservedly ; I should not wish even to hint a suspicion of the honour of the eminent and justly esteemed men by whom all our important examinations are conducted. Suppose that a paper of questions has been drawn up by one person, and that the answers are then put into the hands of another person to examine, who has himself private pupils among the candidates : I do not doubt that the utmost reliance may be placed on the integrity of the examiner, so that practically all the candidates may be considered to be on common ground. I suspect that many persons who look only for a moment at the point now under discussion, implicitly make the supposition here stated, and naturally and rightly are content with the conclusion which I have admitted. But now take a more common case; suppose, as usually happens, that the questions are themselves set by the person who is to examine the answers. It is surely not unreasonable to think that a pupil who has been on intimate terms with an examiner may conjecture with some probability the style and the subject of his questions; in other words the candidate thus favourably circumstanced may be able to guess with some confidence what is likely to be set. As to the extent of the start thus given to the fortunate candidates, there may be diversity of opinion; I do not wish to estimate it too highly, but I am convinced that it has a real existence and value. Indeed, a teacher who has to examine a body composed of his own pupils and others, must feel himself sometimes perplexed by the conflict of duties; if he sets the points which are in his judgment most important, and to which he has naturally invited the special attention of his own pupils, he runs the risk of unfairness to the others; whereas, if he avoids all those specialities he may appear not so much an incompetent as a treacherous guide of those who had confided their interests to him. However, without delaying longer on this consideration, I will pass to another which so far as I know has in general escaped notice, though I venture to consider it of decisive significance. I say then that the fortunate candidate will know in many cases with tolerable certainty, what will *not* be set, and thus will be able to concentrate his attention on a narrower range of matter. Let me explain. In many of the higher departments of mathematics, we have two or three distinct works, readily accessible, each of which naturally has its own peculiarities as to its methods and its extent. Now, if a student has no information to guide him, he will not consider himself safe unless he becomes acquainted with all the ordinary books which treat on a given subject. But should he know that his examiner has not read, or does not esteem, a particular book, then he may without hesitation omit that book from his list, and by confining himself to the remainder can easily surpass, in the subjects thus limited, a rival whose attention has been more widely dispersed. Moreover, the remark applies not only to distinct books, but to different parts of the same book. A private tutor generally indicates in the more elaborate works what he considers the essential parts which are to be carefully mastered, and what he considers of less importance, which may therefore be studied slightly or entirely omitted. Then the candidate who is thus guided as to what he may practically neglect is enabled to strengthen his acquaintance with what is likely to be set.

There is a matter in connexion with examinations, especially at the Universities, which I think ought to be considered and settled on some uniform rule ; and that is the extent of detail with which the results are published. Theoretically, in our competitive examinations the names of the successful candidates are made known in order of merit, but not the number of marks which each has gained. But of late years a practice seems to have sprung up of communicating freely additional information to all enquirers, so that reports, perhaps only partially accurate, are circulated respecting the whole numerical results. I should like to have either authorised publication, or entire reserve; and of the two I prefer the latter. I think the examination ought to be considered a confidential transaction; and that there should be no betrayal of the blunders into which even an able candidate may easily fall in the hurry and excitement of his work. There is good ground for believing that in some cases in which an examination has been not competitive, but merely qualifying, and unsuspecting candidates have been content with passing, and have made no special effort at distinction, the marks have been preserved and have been made to tell unfavourably against those who had reached only a low standard. In such a case, I hold the candidates were treated harshly; no warning had been given to them that the testimony of their papers would ever be used against them, and thus they had not been stimulated to any vigorous exertion.

I cannot however dismiss the subject without adverting to the undue importance which is attached to competitive examinations. For mere boyish proficiency in Classics, that is, speaking generally, for merit which consists largely in having been sent when young to a good school, a fellowship of three or four hundred pounds a year is sometimes awarded. The prize seems to me too great to be made to depend on such a precarious method of appreciating claims as even the best examination furnishes. The large rewards thus held out for attainments in certain studies, estimated in a certain way, tend to make our students regard too much the immediate market value of their knowledge, and to neglect any pursuit which does not promise an early pecuniary return. Hence, we suffer under a disheartening want of faith in all but the mercenary inducements to mental exertion. When any branch of literature or science seems to be inadequately cultivated at the University, and some enthusiasts try to produce an interest in the neglected subject, it is never by the ordinary means of able teaching that we propose to afford the required stimulus and encouragement : the universal remedy is to *put the subject into the examinations.* It is obvious that the subject may possibly be well adapted for private study, or for lecture-room illustration, and very ill adapted for the ordinary process of examination ; but this does not affect us : we prolong our examination schemes, already too extensive, by introducing the fashionable novelty of the period, and soon fall into altercation as to whether or not sufficient bribes are offered in the way of scholarships and fellowships to allure students into the newly opened path.

Again, I should desire to protest strongly against the tendency to prolong examinations beyond the period of youth and very early manhood. Under the present system, a student who takes his B.A. degree at the normal age of about twenty one years, may, I think be held to have been sufficiently tried by examinations. Nevertheless, it is usual to spend two or three more years in reading for a fellowship until either the end is gained, or the chance is found to be too slender to encourage further effort. I regard this part of the University system as an unmixed evil. The examina-

tion for a fellowship is of the same kind as the various
University examinations, so that preparation for it
consists only in prolonging the same training to which
the student has already for many years been subjected;
the staff of examiners, composed of the members of a
single college, cannot, to say the least, be deemed
superior to the University examiners who are selected
from all the colleges. Besides its other disadvantages,
there is the strong objection that this system is unduly
favourable to those who have already some private
resources, and are therefore less in need of a fellowship.
It is obvious, that of two nearly equal competitors,
if one can afford to prolong his training for examination
and the other cannot, the former must ultimately conquer the latter in the contest for academic emoluments.
In fact the rich receive the benefits and the poor are
sent empty away.

As I object to the continuance of examinations far
into the years of manhood, so also I regret to see this
discipline commenced at too early an age. We may
almost say that children are now prepared for com-
petitions in which exhibitions or other school advantages are held out as the prizes of success. One is
tempted to wish that a clause could be inserted in
some Factory Act to control and regulate this variety
of juvenile labour. Human beings, as well as horses,
should be kept clear of the risk of exhausting their
strength in premature races.

But though I see much to dislike in the prevalence
of the system of competitive examinations, I cannot
join in the vituperation which is frequently thrown on
this mode of selecting occupants for subordinate ap-

pointments. Whatever may be said against this method
there is at least an absence of jobbery and corruption
which alone forms a superlative merit. The objections
which are urged in perpetual articles, in journals and
magazines, seem to me objections rather against details
than against the principle. Schemes of examination
may be in some respects injudicious; then let the
necessary improvements be made. We are sometimes
told that this or that qualification is required which
is not guaranteed by proficiency in examinations. The
answer is simple : state the mode in which you would
secure this qualification if there were no competitive
examination; then, if that mode would really succeed,
let it be adopted as an addition to our present competitive process   I should like however to see some
attempt made to institute a fair comparison between
the competitive mode of selection now adopted and
that previously used for various definite appointments,
as for example, the admission to the military academy
at Woolwich, compared with the admission formerly
to Woolwich and to Addiscombe. These would be
good examples, because it may be admitted that the
old system worked reasonably well in these cases.   I
have had some opportunity myself of making a comparison, and my judgment is decidedly in favour of the
present system.

I am aware that many persons think the matter
is settled by asserting that all we do by our examination system, is to encourage *cram;* but unfortunately
no definition is given of what is reprobated by this
much employed word.   It seems to me that at least
one very prominent tendency of the competitive system

is extremely valuable; namely, that of securing from the teacher attention to the progress of his pupils individually. It is very easy in a school or in a professor's lecture room, to lose sight of all except two or three of the more advanced members of the class; so that in effect the instruction may be given principally to those who least require it : but the private teacher who has to prepare each of his pupils against some examination, must endeavour to make the best even of the least promising materials. The main reproach to many of our large schools seems to me to be that a boy of only average ability can so easily avoid all the ameliorating influences of education; and it is to be wished that something could be done to diminish the frequency of such cases. But the merits and faults of school arrangements cannot be discussed at the end of an Essay.

PRIVATE STUDY OF MATHEMATICS.

I HAVE been frequently requested to answer questions and to give advice with respect to mathematical studies by persons who have no teacher; and I am willing to hope that there may be some advantage in collecting the principal reflections which have at various times suggested themselves to me.

The study of mathematics certainly requires steady perseverance in combating with difficulties; but the processes employed and the results to which they lead are both so important and so interesting, that it is not surprising that the pursuit is found eminently inviting. We must not attempt to disguise the fact that if it be the ambition of the student to distinguish himself in one of the numerous stringent examinations which now invite him from every side, he must make up his mind to severe and long-continued exertion. The memory must be trained to preserve a large stock of formulæ and demonstrations; and this alone is a heavy task, because there is none of that aid which the ear would lend to the labour of mastering such prose or poetry as the student of a language might find it necessary to learn. But the repulsive part of mathematics is almost confined to that which is necessary for examination purposes; leaving this out of view for the present, I doubt if the path in mathematical science is more rugged than that which is trodden by the student of a dead language.

Let me at the outset record my opinion of the value of mathematics; I cannot do this better than by adopting the words of Sir J. Herschel, to the influence of which I gratefully attribute the direction of my own early studies. The words are deserving of serious attention, as proceeding from one whose taste and ability had conducted him through the encyclopædia of human knowledge; and I venture to think that at the present time they are at least as applicable as when they were addressed to a preceding generation. Sir J. Herschel says of Astronomy, "Admission to its sanctuary, and to the privileges and feelings of a votary, is only to be gained by one means,—*sound and sufficient knowledge of mathematics, the great instrument of all exact inquiry, without which no man can ever make such advances in this or any other of the higher departments of science as can entitle him to form an independent opinion on any subject of discussion within their range.*"

No person who may consult these pages for guidance in his studies is likely to be without some practical knowledge of Arithmetic; and though it may not be very elaborate, yet it will probably be sufficient. Books containing large stores of examples, with more or less of explanation, are common and need not be specifically mentioned. Those however in which the exhibition of the principles is made the chief object, almost to the exclusion of examples, are not so numerous: one which I may recommend as well suited for the private student, on account of its simplicity and clearness, is the volume published by the late Dr Lardner in his *Cabinet Cyclopædia.*

Practically the study of illustrative mathematics will usually commence with Algebra. I assume that the beginner is fortunate in the text-book which he selects; that he will procure one which has the advantage of proceeding from an author of some scientific reputation. This remark deserves especial attention by those who intend to proceed to the higher parts of mathematics; for ultimate success will depend very much on the early steps. It is obvious that a writer who is himself familiar with mathematical science will be able in writing an elementary book to make provision for the future advantage of his readers, which cannot be supplied by one who has himself scarcely proceeded beyond the range of that book.

No doubt as to the method of study, different teachers might give different advice; and I should be sorry to appear to insist on any recommendation of my own as essential and indispensable: I shall merely propose for the consideration of others what is suggested by my own experience, and especially by the experience gained in watching closely the progress of some who by private study have gained considerable reputation.

I say, then, that the student should read his author with the most sustained attention, in order to discover the meaning of every sentence. If the book is well written, it will endure and repay this close examination: the text ought to be fairly intelligible, even without illustrative examples. Often, far too often, a reader hurries over the text without any sincere and vigorous effort to understand it; and rushes to some example to clear up what ought not to have been obscure, if it had been adequately considered. The habit of scrupulously investigating the text seems to me important on several grounds. The close scrutiny of language is a very valuable exercise both for studious and practical life. In the higher departments of mathematics the habit is indispensable; in the long investigations which occur there it would be impossible to interpose illustrative examples at every stage, the student must therefore encounter and master, sentence by sentence, an extensive and complicated argument.

I venture to think that teachers are occasionally at fault in their mode of treating the difficulties brought under their notice by their pupils. Instead of going through the passage in the text-book carefully with the pupil, in order to see where the difficulty lies, they sometimes put the text-book aside and proceed to the required result by some other way: this may be fairly described as eluding the difficulty rather than surmounting it.

I suppose the student, then, to read his author with close and sustained attention. Of course it must happen that in some cases the author is not understood, or is very imperfectly understood; and the question is what is to be done. After giving a reasonable amount of attention to the passage, let the student pass on, reserving the obscurity for future efforts. If the text-book has been well arranged, in separate independent chapters, it will be generally found that if a few difficult passages in one chapter are left unconquered, still some progress can be made in the subsequent chapters. After a time the student, having left behind him several points not cleared up, will find that he is no longer proceeding with satisfaction to himself; he must then turn back and begin again at the beginning. It will commonly happen that in the revision of the work some of the former difficulties will disappear, and the student will be able to carry his reading beyond the point at which he formerly turned back. The process should be repeated until the whole work is mastered, or at least such parts as may be pointed out for a first course.

It might be conjectured perhaps that this advice is likely to be abused by the student in such a manner as to lead him to give up a difficulty after only a very faint attempt to overcome it; but practically I think that the danger is but slight. The natural tendency of solitary students, I believe, is not to hurry away prematurely from a hard passage, but to hang far too long over it; the just pride that does not like to acknowledge defeat, and the strong will that cannot endure to be thwarted, both urge to a continuance of effort even when success seems hopeless. It is only by experience we gain the conviction that when the mind is thoroughly fatigued it has neither power to continue with advantage its course in an assigned direction, nor elasticity to strike out a new path; but that, on the other hand, after being withdrawn for a time from the pursuit, it may return and gain the desired end.

Perhaps the great embarrassment to beginners however is, not the obscurity of definite isolated passages, but the inability to discover what is the general drift of the processes, and consequently too often a want of faith as to the existence of any distinct object to be attained. I know of no remedy for this depression of mind except the reflection that many men, not a few of whom are held to be illustrious, have prosecuted these studies, have found them permanently attractive, and have used them for most important ends. The passage which I have quoted from Herschel, to which others of a like nature from writers of scarcely inferior reputation might easily be added, will have a significant value in this connexion. Some words attributed to Lagrange himself are still more impressive for our purpose. To encourage students desponding in the early stages of their course he was accustomed to say, "Allez en avant; la foi vous viendra." Often indeed has the story been cited of the good saint who walked a mile with his head chopped off, and found *only* the first step difficult; but I think there is nothing to which the obvious moral is more applicable than to the study of mathematics. The same perplexity is apt to bewilder the student when he enters upon any of the main divisions of the general subject, and must be alleviated by the same prescription. Take for example the Differential Calculus; here the introductory conceptions are so novel, that a student, even if he remembers his temporary despondence, and his final relief in Algebra and Coordinate Geometry, is likely to sink almost into despair. Still the advice must be: go on, and rest assured that the nature of the apparently unmeaning preliminaries will ultimately be understood and appreciated. I have had the satisfaction of finding that advice of this character, which I have offered in one of my mathematical books, has been followed by the most satisfactory results.

A few words may be devoted to the order in which the various branches of mathematics should be taken. After Algebra should follow Plane Trigonometry, and then Plane Coordinate Geometry. The latter subject however has received such enormous extensions in recent years, that it is necessary to address a caution to beginners to prevent them from giving an exorbitant amount of time to developments which however elegant cannot be considered as of essential importance. The elaborate discussion of the modern methods of abridged notation should be reserved at least until a reasonable acquaintance has been made with the Differential and Integral Calculus, and Analytical Mechanics. Great care is necessary in commencing the study of Mechanics; the subject appears to be extremely interesting to most persons, but it is fatally easy to acquire incorrect notions and phrases which will afterwards cause serious trouble. Many ordinary popular works, which are readily accessible, are very deficient in clearness and accuracy of expression; and the beginner cannot be too strongly recommended to be cautious in the selection of his guide in this subject.

There is one peculiarity which is frequently strongly developed in solitary students, namely the desire to engage in independent researches and to effect discoveries while still in only the elementary stage of knowledge. Persons who by accidents of position or of authorship have become even slightly known as of some authority in science receive a large number of communications inviting attention to supposed valuable results obtained by self-taught men. Many such have fallen under my notice; and for the most part they may be arranged in three classes. In the first place we have formulæ offered which are obviously implied in well known propositions, consisting often of only a slight modification in expression. In the next place solutions of problems may be presented in which some implied restriction, which constituted the whole difficulty and interest, is neglected; for instance trigonometry may be employed when an exercise in pure geometry was intended. In the third place results may be sometimes obtained by patient use of elementary resources which follow immediately by the aid of some principles lying a little beyond the elements with which alone the student is familiar. The first class of cases is troublesome to those who are requested to pronounce an opinion on them; it is difficult to convince an enthusiast with little knowledge that what seems to him a novelty is completely involved in the old theorems. The last class of cases is perplexing for another reason. The patience and determination which are sometimes exhibited seem to demand encouragement; and yet a careful judge must hesitate before he ventures to commend. In the first place the result may have been produced by such an expenditure of thought and time as must be pronounced exorbitant, when compared with what the student has at his command. In the second place in the present state of science there is little hope that valuable discoveries can be made by irregular excursions of persons with inadequate knowledge. If a student is pursuing his researches merely for the enjoyment which they yield to himself he may be abundantly gratified by obtaining results which are new to him though well known to others; but if he aspires to add something of permanent value to the stores of knowledge he must begin by making himself well acquainted with the extent of those stores. It would be rash to say that nothing remains for discovery or improvement even in the elements of mathematics; but it may be safely asserted that the ground has been so long and so thoroughly explored as to hold out little hope of profitable return for a casual adventurer.

It has been my uniform practice then to receive the communication of supposed discoveries from zealous beginners in one way, namely by exhortation to the earnest study of the best elementary works, and recommendation to gain an adequate basis of knowledge before engaging on original research. Such advice is of course natural from a writer and a teacher; I trust I have always given it with due consideration for the feelings of my unknown correspondents, and with such praise as I could honestly bestow on any promise which I might discern of future success. A very extreme instance of the habit of solitary students of attaching undue importance to their own supposed discoveries may be seen in the sketch of the life of John Walsh of Cork, by the late Professor Boole; see the Philosophical Magazine for Nov. 1851. The melancholy interest of the story, told with rare beauty of thought and language, cannot fail to produce a deep impression on those who may be brought into contact with buoyant, self-confident, but ill-informed inventors, and to prove that salutary checks may shew truer kindness than injudicious encouragement.

Even the great masters in science must keep themselves well acquainted with the researches of their predecessors and contemporaries if they wish to exert their own powers in the most economical and productive manner: this point is well enforced by Arago in his life of Poisson, who was conspicuous for the extent of his knowledge, and consequently for the effectiveness of his own researches.

I come now to a very important point, namely the solution of examples. I hear repeatedly from solitary students that although they believe they understand what they read in an ordinary Cambridge book of good reputation, yet they find themselves completely baffled by the exercises and problems, to their very great discouragement. The answer which I give to such complaints is substantially this: do not trouble yourselves with the examples, make it your main business, I might almost say your exclusive business, to understand the text of your author.

The large collection of examples which our modern Cambridge books supply will be found to be almost an exclusive peculiarity of these books; such collections scarcely exist in foreign treatises on mathematics, nor even in English treatises of an earlier date. This fact shews I think that a knowledge of mathematics may be gained without the perpetual working of examples. The great increase of competitive examinations in this country however, has led to the devotion of a large amount of time and attention on the part of examiners to the construction of ingenious exercises and problems; the performance of any feat of skill becomes easy by long practice, and thus we need not wonder that the habit of producing elegant examination papers has been carried to marvellous perfection at Cambridge. We hear students from other places who occasionally resort to our private tutors, declare that with themselves they have no men who can either make a problem or solve a problem; and the superiority of Cambridge in this point is well indicated by the implied compliment. There can be no doubt that for variety, novelty, and beauty, the papers set at our College and University examinations far surpass any others in the world. In fact the fertility of invention and combination which these papers exhibit would astonish any competent judge whom custom had not rendered familiarly acquainted with them.

The increasing severity of our examinations renders it necessary to commence the study of Mathematics at an earlier age than was usual formerly; and thus it happens that even in the books constructed for beginners we have a large supply of varied examples. Of course a student who has sufficient resolution to undertake the pursuit of mathematics without a teacher may be trusted to decide for himself whether he understands his author or not; but with youth who need some external restraint to keep them diligent the only mode of testing whether they understand the theory or not is to set them some examples to work.

Now experience shews us that the power of solving mathematical problems is drawn out, I might almost say is created, by practice; and the practice must be long and assiduous before any decided success can be gained. The nature of a problem and the mode in which many problems are really constructed might lead us to anticipate that such would be the case.

There are a large number of elementary facts and principles in pure and mixed mathematics; in general a problem consists mainly of the combination of two or more such elements. For an illustration take the following: if three particles be projected at the same instant and left to the action of gravity, the plane which passes through them at any instant always remains parallel to itself; the result is easily shewn to follow from an elementary fact in geometry combined with two elementary facts in mechanics. In many cases if the precise combination which was present to the mind of the framer can be seized, the solution is obvious and rapid; but if his combination does not present itself the solution may be long and intricate, or even impracticable. Now it may be readily supposed that the faculty of rapidly reviewing the store of elementary facts, and of selecting a promising combination out of the inexhaustible number that could be formed, is at first dormant even if it be innate, and needs incessant cultivation to become conspicuous.

A good teacher will be of immense service in guiding and training students to solve problems; he will draw attention to the most important and most fertile principles, and reiterate the illustrations of points that seem inadequately grasped. Solitary students must resign themselves to the admission of the superior advantages of their more fortunate competitors; but I am persuaded it is the most economical plan for such solitary students to devote their energies almost entirely to the study of their text-books, and not to exhaust themselves in perpetual struggles with problems. By continuing their reading they will gradually become familiar with the processes by which problems are solved; the inventive faculty may be developed somewhat later than is common with those who are trained by a tutor, but ultimately it may be not less vigorous.

I am at present considering a student of mathematics for its own sake—not for examination purposes. A person who intends to offer himself for an examination must, in common prudence, prepare himself for the special demands of that examination; and one of the most stringent of these, at least where the influence of Cambridge predominates, is the solution of problems. Although I have expressed my admiration of the high quality of many of these problems, yet it must not be supposed that I view with entire satisfaction the lavish expenditure of time and ability which is involved in their construction. And it may be questioned whether the habit of problem solving, which our competitive examinations develope, is necessarily of supreme value either as a general training or as a special cultivation of mathematical power. I have sometimes asserted that we train our students to think with sustained vigour on a given point for about the space of twenty minutes. If a candidate has devoted more than this to a problem, and is not within a hopeful prospect of the conclusion, he is very probably in the wrong path : he knows this, and naturally shrinks from a further expenditure of time. But the real advances in mathematics, as in other sciences, require frequently the devotion not of minutes but of days or months.

I will venture to allude specially to the collections of examples in my own elementary books, as I have naturally received many communications respecting them.

Sometimes complaints have reached me that the examples are too difficult. Now though many of the examples are original, others have been selected from the various college and university examination papers; so that it may be safely said that they are faithful specimens of what a student who is about to undergo such examinations will have to encounter : in other words, the standard of difficulty is not fixed by the author of the text-book, but by external arrangements over which he has no control. It would be possible to construct examples in abundance which could be solved with almost mechanical certainty by the student; all that is necessary is to make the examples mere repetitions of a few easy types. I remember many years since that an able teacher condemned an elementary book on Algebra, which he had used in a school, on the ground that it was *too easy*. On seeking for an explanation of this apparent paradox, I found that the examples had been carefully adjusted so as to avoid every novelty or difficulty that could occur. It would be a waste of time for youths to run through such a series; the very first actual examination which they experienced would shew that they had been flattered and deceived in supposing that they had acquired any facility in solving such exercises as are actually set. Although this book never came under my own notice, yet I have certainly observed the same characteristic in at least two other elementary mathematical works. The examples were so artfully fabricated as to furnish no material for the occupation of thought and judgment. Examiners however will persist in setting ingenious questions, will in fact propose genuine problems; and against such the spiritless fictions to be found appended to these text-books afforded no preparation.

In the examples which I have borrowed from examination papers I have been careful to preserve the original enunciations of the authors; this is not such a trifling circumstance as may appear at first sight. Every person who has given much attention to authorship must acquire some distinctive characteristic of style; if therefore he moulds all his questions in his own way, he will incur the danger of influencing his readers in such a manner that they may find other forms of expression unusual and perplexing. Thus too great uniformity in the language and composition of the exercises in which a student is trained should be avoided as yielding insufficient warning of the variety which may be exhibited by the questions of examiners. If an alteration were made in the form in which an eminent mathematician has enunciated his problems, there would be at least the appearance of presumption; but even if I have persuaded myself that some improvement could be effected, I have been convinced that for the reason which I have stated it would be wisest to refrain.

Correspondents who have requested from me aid for special problems, have frequently suggested that it would be very advantageous to give hints for the solution of the more difficult examples, or to change them for others of an easier kind. The fatal objection to this recommendation is the want of uniformity of opinion as to which are the more difficult examples. When a paper of problems is proposed at an examination it not unfrequently happens that, although no candidate has solved more than a third of the number, yet every problem has been solved by one or more : what appeared hard and repulsive to one has been found easy and attractive by another, and no two candidates perhaps would arrange the paper in the same order of difficulty. I have found myself that although I have been repeatedly asked for hints as to the solution of examples, yet there has been extremely little tendency to agreement in the selection of the difficult cases, except where there may have unfortunately been some misprint.

I hope there is not adequate foundation for an opinion which I once heard from an ingenious pupil of my own. I found him engaged in solving some examples selected by himself ; and I observed that he invariably avoided those for the treatment of which some hint had been supplied in the book. He said he was sure that unless there had been some special difficulty no hint would have been supplied, and he suspected that even with the hint the example would not be reduced to the average level of practicability. I may remark here incidentally that when private students have not time or have not inclination to work steadily through a collection of some examples, but yet desire some exercise of the kind, I always recommend them to follow some rigid rule, such as that of taking the first third of the set, or of taking every third example. If a student allows himself an arbitrary license of selection he naturally chooses those examples which for some reason appear most attractive to him ; and very probably he thus takes those which really he least requires.

Sometimes the suggestion has been made that a representative example of each of the more usual kinds should be solved fully in the text-book at the end of every chapter. The variety of exercises which can be constructed is however so great that it would be impossible within any moderate compass to include representatives of all the types which can occur. Moreover the attempt would I believe to some extent cause its own failure. There is in fact a ceaseless struggle going on, perhaps unconsciously, between teachers and examiners ; the former wish to anticipate what is likely to appear, and to prepare their pupils for it; the latter strive for ingenious novelties by which to test the power of the candidate and the quality of the instruction he has received. Thus if an elementary book lays stress on a particular kind of problem, we may safely predict that the instinct of an examiner will lead him to avoid this point and seek for some other which he may expect to find less elaborately guarded.

Printed solutions of examples seem to be found uninteresting judging from the difficulty in persuading at least the younger students to read them. But much benefit may be derived by a judicious use of such works especially by those who have not the assistance of a tutor. I need scarcely say that a vigorous effort should be made to obtain the solution without the book; and particular attention should be given to discover the cause of failure when the book is consulted. Solitary students generally are slow in apprehending all the

T.   6

conventions which are implicitly regarded in the enunciation of problems; their general tendency is to understand the problem in some wider or more difficult sense than was designed: the use of a good collection of solutions is then of great assistance in gaining a familiarity with the precise force of the language in which examples are proposed.

One striking peculiarity of mathematics is its unlimited power of evolving examples and problems. A student may read through a book of Euclid, or a few chapters of Algebra; and within that limited range of knowledge it is possible to set him exercises as real and as interesting as the propositions themselves which he has studied; deductions which might have pleased the Greek geometers, and algebraical properties which Pascal and Fermat would not have disdained to investigate. Contrast this with what takes place in other studies. A beginner we may say spends months on his Latin Grammar and his Latin Delectus; and then all that he can have by way of exercise is a collection of such trifling statements as, *the bird sings, the dog barks,* which he has to turn into Latin. It seems to me that a student of language will in general have to go through years of labour before his powers can be tested by any thing corresponding in freshness and reality to the problems which can be proposed almost to beginners in mathematics.

Perhaps however the great excellence of the problems in Mathematics sometimes leads teachers to underestimate the amount of patience and ingenuity required to solve them; thus pupils are expected to succeed nearly uniformly when it would be more reasonable to be satisfied if they did not uniformly fail. A very acute critic and able teacher in the course of a correspondence on elementary mathematics remarked to me "Would you not consider it a heavy charge against your Algebra if the school-boys after reading the Chapters failed to do the examples?" My correspondent wished to establish that Euclid is a bad book for the purposes of elementary instruction because boys when taught from this book were according to his experience very inexpert in the treatment of problems and deductions. My reply was that I am never surprised to find beginners slow in such operations; what they are thus required to perform is really of the nature of original work, and we must be content to find the inventive faculty weak at first, though it may be susceptible of large development under the influence of judicious training.

Let me make one remark for the use of those who may have the opportunity of occasional recourse to a teacher; they should endeavour to put the difficulty in a precise and definite form. If an experienced teacher can be personally consulted he will in general be able to discover by a few judicious questions the point of difficulty; but where a letter is the channel of intercourse the enquirer should himself do more: he must endeavour to shew distinctly what he wishes to have explained. Perhaps an assertion is made for which he can see no warrant; or there may be an apparent contradiction between two statements; or some principle adopted in the subject seems to lead to an untenable inference. If only the obstacle is distinctly pointed out there may be but little trouble in

removing it. But if there is merely a general remark
that a certain article or chapter is very perplexing,
then as there is no exact description of the complaint
it is impossible to supply a remedy. A late very eminent mathematician was accustomed to require written
applications for explanation even from pupils with
whom he was in daily contact: he maintained that the
supposed difficulty often disappeared under the effort
of describing it accurately.

Similarly with respect to the solution of a problem;
when requested to furnish one I always desire if possible to see the attempt which has been made and
has failed. However slight such an attempt may be,
it in general suggests what will be the most instructive method of guiding the student in the particular
case : and without such a hint the solution presented
may be of very little educational advantage.

But let me now suppose that our self-taught mathematician intends to offer himself for some public examination. Although I think it impossible for him to
have an equal chance of distinction with candidates
specially trained by a tutor whom long practice has
rendered skilful in his profession; yet there are at least
some general considerations which may be of service
in improving the position of the solitary student. I
am conscious that these remarks may seem so obvious
as to render it superfluous to record them; but I have
learned by experience and frequent correspondence
that the most simple and self-evident maxims escape
the notice of those who are not practically familiar with
the exigencies of examinations.

I say then that the first and most imperative obli-

gation of the candidate is to endeavour to ascertain
the nature and the range of the examination by consulting the papers which have been recently set at
the College or University to which he is about to proceed in the particular subject which he is preparing.
It is not sufficient to consult merely the official programmes. Suppose for example that we find *Algebra*
named in a programme; we should still require to
know how much is included under this title. One
examining board might draw the line at quadratic
equations; another might extend the limits so as to
involve large parts of the Theory of Numbers, the
Theory of Probability, and the Theory of Equations.
Besides the uncertainty as to the extent of the subjects
there is also room for extreme diversity in the character
of the questions set. One examination may consist
mainly or entirely of book-work; that is of propositions taken directly from the elementary treatises: in
another examination problems and exercises may constitute the predominant element. It is obvious that
the modes of preparation must vary with the nature
and the extent of the examination papers; and hence
it is most imprudent for a candidate to present himself
for a trial if he has neglected to acquaint himself with
the essential conditions under which that trial will be
conducted. But I regret to say that a precaution so
simple, and so obviously demanded by common sense,
is frequently altogether disregarded.

Here I may apparently digress, but really I shall I
hope impress the point more strongly, if I draw attention to two extremes as to the constitution of examinations.

Take for example on the one hand the examinations for mathematical honours at Cambridge; here it may be said that the utmost liberty exists: the examiners are scarcely fettered in any manner as to the difficulty of their problems, or the value to be assigned to them. The examiners are in fact independent; there is no authority which in any way controls their action. Thus the papers may vary considerably from year to year; there may be for some period a run as it were on certain subjects followed by a comparative neglect of them. Undoubtedly then here there must be some precariousness; that is to say it is conceivable that a particular set of papers has been favourable to a certain individual and unfavourable to another; and that a slightly different order of position might have been obtained on any assigned occasion if the papers had been exchanged for those of another year.

On the other hand where there is an official programme which is very strictly maintained it becomes in some measure possible to conjecture what a forthcoming examination paper will contain. Indeed I hold that this power of anticipation may seriously damage the value of the examination as a test of knowledge. It would not be impossible to name certain academic honours which are much deteriorated by the constrained adherence of the examiners to the letter of an official programme. The supreme authority may be vested not in the examiners but in some senate or committee; and this may be composed of men who though formerly or actually eminent in the branches of study which they control, may yet be absolutely destitute of experience as teachers or examiners.

In connexion with this part of my subject I may remark on one peculiarity which exercises an important influence on examinations; it is the comparative fertility or dearth of good exercises. In some departments of science, as for instance the elements of natural philosophy, it is found by no means easy to supply an adequate variety of questions at once sufficiently simple, and yet requiring some employment of thought. The consequence is obvious. If examiners are practically unrestricted they gradually withdraw from the sterile fields and cultivate those which supply a more abundant harvest of problems and exercises. If the examiners are closely confined to the official programme they cannot avoid repeating the available questions, so that a provident tutor may advance a good conjecture as to what is likely to be set.

It is thus sufficiently obvious from what has been said that it is *absolutely necessary* for a person who intends to undergo an examination to make himself well acquainted not only with the official programme but with the commentary on it which the recent examination papers will supply. This does not involve in the slightest degree any attempt to evade the requirements of the prescribed course, but only the just and prudent resolution to ascertain distinctly what is prescribed. I have heard of Academic bodies which formerly attempted to prevent the publication of examination papers, and even compelled the candidates to leave them in the examination room; but I think that all such attempts at mystery are now abandoned. The very fact that examination papers are now rendered so easily accessible sufficiently indicates that the propriety and duty of consulting them is fully admitted.

Let us now suppose that a student has to prepare a particular mathematical subject; and that guided by common report or by the advice of some friend, he has procured a suitable text-book. Now it cannot be too emphatically impressed on the candidate that it is not sufficient for examination purposes to *understand* a proposition; it must in general be *known* so as to be producible at a moment's notice and be written out without hesitation. Solitary students fail very frequently at this point, and the failure is extremely natural; it is so obvious that for a student of mathematics the main thing is to *understand* what he reads, that it is fatally easy to imagine that this will be enough for examination purposes. If unlimited time were allowed it might be possible for an able man to reproduce by continued effort what he had once merely understood; but we know that the hours are strictly counted at an examination, that more questions are usually set than can really be discussed; and thus unless a well-trained memory is at the service of an intellect however acute, the amount produced will be but a small fraction of the required whole. It will be fortunate for the solitary student if by hints derived from the fate of others, or by an unusual effort of sagacity, he discovers what he will otherwise assuredly learn by painful experience, that for examination purposes he must *remember* accurately as well as *comprehend* distinctly.

But then it is plain in looking at the text-books— gradually increasing in number and expanding in bulk —that it is impossible for a person with ordinary power really to *know* all the propositions in any subject. Thus in fact some selection must be made; a pupil will on this point consult his tutor, and rely on his judgment.

Good advice here will be most valuable. If one student attempts to master the whole of a treatise, and another concentrates his attention on the half, suppose, from which questions are usually taken, it is obvious that the latter will be in general twice as well prepared as the former at the points where a trial is likely to be made.

The only method by which very trustworthy information can be gained by the solitary student as to the distinction between the essential and the non-essential parts of a subject is the comparison of examination papers which have been set on previous occasions; but in addition some suggestions may be made which though rather vague will not be quite unserviceable.

Very long and intricate investigations may in general be passed over; and this for a double reason: such investigations are not very likely to be set, and even if they were to appear occasionally yet the difficulty of mastering them, and the probability of failing at some point in the attempt to reproduce them, render it unadvisable to spend much time on them. There are certain propositions which, as tutors of experience know, rarely occupy a place in the papers; but it can hardly be expected that the unassisted student would detect them. If the demonstration is of a very artificial character so that it cannot be easily modified in form; or if the result does not readily admit of deductions and exercises, then the proposition is liable to be much neglected by examiners. The reason is obvious; such a question does not serve to discriminate the candidates. It divides them into two classes; those who wrote out the ordinary demonstration and those who did not, so that neither class offers any gradation in merit. Examiners naturally seek for such propositions as are susceptible of variety in treatment, descending from great excellence by continued transition down to complete failure.

It must be admitted that the neglect of various important propositions because they are intricate and apparently artificial is an evil which belongs to our examination system. I think that examiners might do something to mitigate this evil by occasionally requiring an *outline* of the process of investigation, or the development of some part of it: but still the remedy will be only imperfect. I ought to add that a student really desirous of mathematical knowledge should not completely neglect such propositions; he should read them so far as to understand them, and to remember the result, even if he avoids the labour of learning them thoroughly.

Finally, each individual will probably find that there are propositions which for some reason or other he cannot easily retain in his memory. My advice may seem rather enervating, but I confess that I recommend students to give up such refractory passages. Experience shews that whatever pains may have been taken, the memory is likely to prove treacherous at last; and thus there is the mortification of feeling that an unusual effort has been made, and made in vain. It is an unfortunate peculiarity of a mathematical demonstration that if a single step is forgotten it is impossible to advance; and so long as papers are set with more examples than can be worked in the allotted

time, a candidate may omit some completely, and yet
have his mind and his fingers unceasingly occupied.

I suppose then that a student will confine himself
to those portions of the text-book which his own judgment, or the advice of others, points out as the most
important for examination purposes; yet the caution
is necessary that he should endeavour to obtain a discriminating knowledge of the results obtained in other
portions of the book which he passes over lightly. To
remember what has been demonstrated is often very
serviceable, even if the mode of demonstration has been
forgotten. For suppose that a proposition is set in an
examination, and that a candidate, quite unconscious
that it is a piece of book-work, attacks it as a problem
with his personal resources. In the first place, as in
the case of any problem, he may possibly discover that
all his efforts are fruitless. In the second place, even
if he does achieve something like a solution, it is almost
certain that his process will be very inferior to that of
the text-book; for of course the author of this had
unlimited time, and also access to the labours of his
predecessors. In the third place, although the solution
may have been produced by much thought, and may
really do credit to the original power of the candidate,
yet the examiner cannot appreciate its merit in this
relative manner: he can only award what is due to an
ordinary piece of book-work. Lastly, the enunciations
of the propositions in the text-books are sometimes
rather brief, so that without the commentary which
the investigation furnishes there might be some uncertainty as to the meaning: and consequently the
candidate, to whom it appears in the guise of a pro-

blem, is liable to misapprehend what he is expected to accomplish.

Observation shews that even those who have had the advantage of the best tuition not unfrequently fall into the error of attempting to treat as a problem what is really a forgotten or unknown piece of book-work; and thus we may anticipate that solitary students will be exposed to the same danger. The practical advice is this: distinguish carefully between what is book-work and what is a problem; and except in very special cases do not attempt to supply the lack of memory by the force of invention, that is to say, do not under the restraints of an examination challenge a comparison with the maturer knowledge and ampler leisure of the writer of the popular text-book.

I pass to a point just suggested, namely, the necessity of understanding the questions in the examiner's sense. There may be some ambiguity in the language. Thus, for example, the word *cone* may occur, and it may not be immediately obvious whether the simplest cone is intended, that is, a right circular cone, or some more general form. On the one hand, if the candidate takes the narrowest possible view, he is in danger of avoiding all the real difficulty, and so of falling far below the examiner's requirements. On the other hand, if the candidate takes the widest possible view he is in danger of rendering the problem quite impracticable for his resources, and of attempting far more than was expected. It would seem on the whole the most prudent course to take the problem in the easiest possible meaning which the words will fairly warrant.

But at least in the more elaborate University Examinations there will rarely be questions of which the exact meaning is not apparent on due consideration. It is very customary at Cambridge to append to every book-work question a deduction which is technically called a *rider*. Both the book-work and the rider should be carefully read by a candidate who is anxious to meet precisely the examiner's requirements. Even if, as unfortunately may be the case, the candidate's powers do not allow him to attack the rider with any great confidence of success, yet the consideration of it will often guide him as to the nature of the answer expected for the book-work question. If the rider is disregarded until after the discussion of the book-work, there is sometimes the mortification of seeing plainly that what the examiner wished to be brought prominently forward has been neglected.

It is advisable for candidates to believe that in a careful examination every question has some definite power; and in general also every question will require the expenditure of an average amount of time and of paper. Candidates in escaping from an examination-room may occasionally be heard congratulating themselves and frightening their tutors by some such words as these: "I did that question in half-a-dozen lines." It is highly probable that the examiner himself expected much more than half-a-dozen lines, and that the candidate has completely missed the point of the question.

It might be supposed by a stranger to examination customs that the proper course, in any case of doubt as to the meaning of a question, is to consult the examiner. But, to say nothing of the time which would be consumed in frequent applications of this kind, I may remark that examiners are naturally very little disposed to encourage such petitions for assistance; they may be expected to believe that their own meaning has been adequately expressed, and they may fear to deviate in the slightest degree from strict justice by furnishing a hint towards a solution to the enquiring candidate. I am glad to observe a tendency in all examinations to abstain from alluring the candidates to any personal appeal for explanation.

Perhaps however the tendency to seek for information as to the meaning of the questions is more common among those who have had the advantage of instruction than among solitary students: indeed, the fault of over-explanation is one into which a zealous teacher is very likely to fall. I remember to have observed this characteristic in the instructions of a very able and enthusiastic teacher, whom I did not know personally, but whose pupils came under my notice; they were obviously accustomed to run to him for a commentary on almost every question he proposed to them: indeed I greatly fear that he frequently went so far as to draw a diagram for them on very slight provocation. This however is very debilitating treatment for examination purposes; candidates must be trained in habits of self-reliance, and must learn to extract for themselves the exact meaning of the questions proposed to them. A teacher should cultivate a judicious severity, and remonstrate with his pupils when he finds them perpetually demanding an account of the meaning of the questions; they must be made to see that if they persist in their claim for such assistance they must renounce all pretension to the merit of the solution which they may afterwards obtain.

Suppose that a question admits of more than one meaning, it will be for a candidate to determine whether it is prudent to pass to another question, or to prolong his attention to this. If he remains faithful to the ambiguous question he must select the most probable meaning, and try it; if he finds that this meaning is inconsistent with the results which he obtains as he pursues his investigations he must be prepared to abandon it and try another. Though I hold that every question should be enunciated in the most exact manner, yet I am never very sorry to see a candidate compelled to hesitate and weigh the claims of two conflicting interpretations. Such an exercise seems to me valuable as a training, both for other studies and for the ordinary business of life.

Those who have to acquire their knowledge by their solitary efforts are, I believe, not so liable to be troubled by the possibility of multiple interpretations, as by the inability of seeing more than one admissible meaning. That is, they are liable to attach some one sense to the words, and to hold this tenaciously without the slightest suspicion that it may not be the sense intended. Hence, not unfrequently they conclude that a proposition is untrue when the only fault is that they have misunderstood it. A kind of intellectual flexibility is strongly to be desired for a candidate at an examination. He is in fact to be tested by two or three persons, each of whom may, with respect to attainments and mental power, have a distinctive

individual character; and it is or should be the business
of the candidate to start from the examiner's point, and
to follow his indications. Cases have occurred at Cambridge in which students of conspicuous ability have
failed to do themselves adequate credit at examinations,
and the failure has arisen from a sort of involuntary
stubbornness which prevented them from ready sympathy with the views of their examiners.

I have sometimes observed in pupils a singular
want of the intellectual flexibility of which I am speaking. A student may be set to read a certain subject,
and a paper of questions then proposed to him to test
his comprehension of his work. The questions may be
answered extremely well on the whole, the errors being
few considering the nature of the subject, and the
amount of time given to it. The tutor explains and
corrects the mistakes, and indulges the natural hope
that a pupil who has acquitted himself so creditably on
the first trial will obtain a nearly complete mastery of
the subject on revising his reading. But to the tutor's
dismay he may perhaps find at the end of a few months
when he again examines his pupil that the old errors
are reproduced almost without mitigation. I do not
say that this type of pupils, characterised by the
feebleness of the power of improvement as compared
with that of acquisition is very common, but it has a
real existence. There are minds so tenacious of their
first impressions on any subject that even the errors
cannot be eradicated; and as such cases occur even
among the pupils of eminent tutors, it is not doubtful
that they must be found among those who have not
the advantage of intercourse with others, which is in

general the best remedy for the unyielding stiffness of intellectual solitude.

It must be remembered that notwithstanding the care which is usually bestowed on the composition of an examination paper, a result proposed as an exercise may be wrong; indeed there have been cases, though rare, in which a single set of questions contained several errors. Hence it is necessary to warn the candidate against lavishing too much time upon any single question; there is both the great probability that the matter may be beyond the range of his powers, and there is also the probability, minute indeed but still existing, that the examiner himself has gone astray. There is little likelihood that this advice will be abused, and the candidate induced to abandon every attempt at the slightest appearance of difficulty; the natural tendency of every vigorous mind is to continue its efforts to surmount a formidable obstacle, even when these efforts are apparently hopeless. I do not remember any case of a candidate who regretted that he had too hastily retreated from an unpromising attack; but Cambridge tradition still hands down warnings of the opposite danger, pointing to instances where a slight inaccuracy in the enunciation of a problem or a latent fault in the process of solution lured a candidate on to such an extravagant waste of time as to lose a senior-wranglership.

It is, I fear, not quite superfluous to warn a candidate under examination that he must not expect any error of his to pass undetected. I do not suppose for an instant that any attempt would be made deliberately to mislead or deceive an examiner; but I think I have sometimes seen an ambitious student, conscious of his own ability, half disposed to esteem himself at least equal to his examiners, and to hope that he may, as it were, constrain them to adopt his investigation, or at least to tolerate it without any very severe criticism : but I hold this to be a fatal mistake. Let us assume for the moment that a particular student is superior to a particular examiner in original power, yet nevertheless the advantage is immeasurably on the side of the examiner. To say nothing of greater age and experience, we must remember that the examiner chooses the ground ; out of the whole range of the subject he selects a few points and concentrates his attention on them, so that he can hardly fail to be superior in strength at these points to the candidate who must necessarily have diffused his energy over the whole extent. Moreover, the examiner will in general have the great benefit of discussing the questions at leisure with his colleagues. And finally, the examiner has in general on his side against a single candidate all the other competitors. Sanscrit fabulists tell a story of three rogues who, by their combined assertions, persuaded a Brahmin that a kid which he was carrying on his shoulder for a sacrifice was really a dog, and thus induced the holy man to fling the beast away. So if all the candidates on any occasion combined to favour the same erroneous solution of a question they might stagger a weak examiner ; but in fact, in a competitive struggle, each candidate is striving for the pre-eminence, and so the examiner has all the others to assist him against the seductive errors of an individual.

By a natural transition I may pass to another error

into which those who are preparing for an examination sometimes fall. Suppose that an examiner, by reason of his published works, or by current report, is known to have distinguished himself in the cultivation of a certain branch of mathematics ; then a zealous student may hastily assume that by throwing his strength into this direction he will reap an abundant harvest of marks. Speaking generally, I consider this a dangerous illusion. It is very likely that an examiner who has himself devoted great attention to a special subject will be reluctant rather than eager to bring his own pursuits prominently forward. Moreover, as to the questions which may occur in these specialities, it is possible that his own eminent knowledge may raise his standard of merit. What is familiar to himself, he may naturally think must be easy and ought to be familiar to others; and thus, instead of placing a bounty on his favourite studies by extravagant liberality he may be discouraging them by unconscious parsimony.

Although a candidate should prudently avoid any such distracting consideration of the points as to which the examiners may be supposed to be exceptionally strong, yet he can with advantage endeavour to adjust his preparation relatively to the demands of the programme or the arrangements established by custom. Suppose for instance that two subjects which I will call A and B occur together in a morning paper, and two other subjects, C and D, in an afternoon paper. It is the obvious course of the candidate to make himself well acquainted with *one* of the morning subjects, and with *one* of the afternoon subjects, rather than with the two morning subjects *or* the two afternoon subjects. If he

knows *one* of the morning subjects and *one* of the afternoon subjects it is quite possible that he may find all
his time fully and advantageously occupied ; whereas if
he has devoted himself mainly either to the morning
pair or the afternoon pair, he may be sitting idle on
one occasion, while he finds more than he can get
through on the other.

Some candidates at an examination indulge in the
practice of performing much rough work on auxiliary
pieces of paper, which they do not send up to the
examiner ; so at the close of the prescribed time their
place is indicated by a heap of scraps and fragments.
The practice is not to be commended.   Work done like
this on waste paper is very likely to be done inaccu-
rately, and to have to be repeated.   For examination
purposes the habit should be cultivated of writing out
every thing continuously and exactly, with the view of
submitting it to the inspection of the examiner ; and
with respect to future occupations in life it is most
important to acquire the faculty of accurate and uninterrupted expression.   I wish that in estimating the
merits of candidates we could take into account not
merely the amount of correct matter that may remain
after erasures and cancels, but also the absence of these
tokens of infirmity.   It is certainly high merit to have
sent up a large number of well-filled sheets, and it is
an increase of that merit if few or no spoiled sheets are
left behind.

Some uncertainty may remain on a subordinate
point as to the most profitable mode of employing the
time in an examination-room.   One candidate may
prefer to write out first all that he feels confident

about, so that he will confine himself to the book-work until he has finished it, and then proceed to consider some of the riders. Another candidate may endeavour to complete one question with its rider before passing to another. I prefer to recommend the latter course. Students who adopt the former are exposed to the danger of exhausting their time and themselves on the book-work, without ever approaching the riders which are naturally the most searching and the most liberally rewarded part. Moreover, as I have already said, by the careful reading and scrutiny of the rider, light is usually thrown on the precise meaning of the book-work question.

I have been much surprised to observe that many students fail to notice the important distinction between working at a paper for a teacher and for an examiner. The main object to be attained is very different in the two cases. In submitting a paper to a private tutor or a lecturer the object is to gain instruction; in leaving them to the judgment of an examiner the object is to secure marks. Hence it may be a salutary rule in the latter case to avoid hazardous experiments, and to write out for the most part what is known, before proceeding to questions in which success is very uncertain. But students in a lecture-room or engaged with a private tutor often proceed as if they were involved in an examination, and so were directing their efforts to secure the highest score of marks. Prudence, however, would suggest the wiser course of trying for the criticism of the private tutor or lecturer the questions which may be imperfectly known rather than those which are well known. Or it may be a judicious rule to try the questions in order, omitting all those which are consciously familiar. However, it is unnecessary to dwell on the point, for it is obvious that a student should reveal his ignorance to his teacher in order that it may be dispelled, and display his knowledge to his examiner in order that it may be rewarded.

A caution on an apparently trivial matter must not be omitted. The candidate must really endeavour to write legibly, and must not indulge in abbreviations which are not fully admitted by custom. Frequently from inordinate haste the writing is so bad that it is almost illegible. Candidates seem to think that an examiner is bound to decipher any obscure scrawl that is put before him, but a little consideration will shew that this notion of an examiner's duty is unreasonable and impracticable. It may be said to be a standing rule in all examinations that the results should be published after the lapse of a definite interval; so that the examiner has only a fixed time, never extravagantly long, to devote to his work. It may be that for a certain set of papers he can assign on an average half an hour to each candidate. It follows then that he cannot give to particular individuals more than their due share of his attention, for by doing so he would defraud the others. There can be but one result. What is illegible after a fair amount of trouble has been expended upon it must be rejected without appreciation; that is, must be treated as if there had been no pretence at writing it. Again, unless candidates are careful to abstain from unrecognised abbreviations they are liable to fall into the habit of writing a species of short hand, mutilating many of the words, and omitting some altogether. A just examiner has but one course open to him; assuming that he can understand the half-expressed meaning, yet he must keep back from the candidate such a percentage of marks as may correspond to the time which has been thus surreptitiously appropriated.

Finally I will repeat, what indeed I have already implied, that the endeavour must be made to answer exactly what is set. It is in vain to expect that the examiner will be compassionate and give marks for the voluntary exhibition of something which may be allied to what he requires, but is not the thing itself. This caution indeed applies to every kind of examination, and Cambridge traditions enforce the remark in various ways. They tell of a youth who, being quite unable to satisfy his examiners as to a problem, endeavoured to mollify them as he said "by writing out book-work bordering on the problem." They tell of another who was rejected, and who challenged the unfavourable decision in such words as these: "if there had been fairer examiners and better papers I should have passed; I knew many things which were not set."

ACADEMICAL REFORM.

In former times an institution might continue to exist unmolested for years or for generations after it had ceased to put forth any blossom or to perfect any fruit; but at present nothing remains long unchallenged. It is not sufficient to be respectable and harmless; unless some positively advantageous results can be brought into evidence no security can be felt for the most ancient and most venerable foundations. We cannot wonder then that Universities, like constitutional government, should now be put on their trial.

The revenues of the Universities and Colleges will soon be known with accuracy; but we can hardly suppose that the aggregate for each University is less than a quarter of a million of pounds annually. Can we say that the benefits secured to literature and to science are commensurate with this amount? University reformers would probably assert with confidence that they are not; and in consequence they would recommend various methods of turning the revenues to better account.

Let us then advert to some of the proposals for what in the language of railways might be called augmenting the dividend or reducing the working expenses.

My remarks of course are intended to apply principally to the University of Cambridge.

I will first consider the Clerical Fellowships. Many of the fellowships at Cambridge are forfeited at the end of an assigned number of years unless the fellow has taken orders in the English Church. This regulation is condemned by objectors because on the one hand it offers a bribe by which a man may be urged to become a clergyman without any real inclination for such an office, and even with a positive repugnance to the engagements which he thus undertakes; and on the other hand able men who might shine in literature and science are lost to their University because they decline to promise what they feel it will be irksome to perform. It may be added that in some cases, I will not say in many, the rule has deterred a person of scrupulous conscience from entering on duties which he might really have been well qualified to discharge; conscious that there was a large reward in position, dignity, and influence thus tempting him, he has shrunk from contemplating a step which might seem in any degree prompted by sordid motives. It has been said that no Irish Catholic would condescend to listen to any argument against his religion as long as that religion was under persecution; and in like manner men have sometimes feared to entertain the thought of taking sacred orders because of the potent temptation to do so.

But we must not lay any great stress on these somewhat speculative considerations; in every station and at every time of life men must have to decide between the seductions of apparent interest and the monitions of conscience and must accept the responsibility of the course they take. Many years since two students met by accident at the Inner Temple in London, both engaged in the regular method of qualifying for the English bar; one of them referring to a recent transaction in his own college exclaimed indignantly: "What a shame it is to compel a man distinguished for his ability and attainments to take orders against his wish in order to retain his fellowship!" The other replied very effectively: "But surely a man of so much power might have given up his fellowship and earned his living without forcing his conscience." It becomes painfully manifest in the course of time that in some cases sacred orders have been rashly taken.

Leaving however all precarious ground let us attempt to give a practical foundation to the discussion. I do not suppose that it would be possible to defend the exclusive clerical fellowships, except on the following grounds:—1. That by this means a succession of learned theologians is preserved. 2. That by this means a supply of laborious and earnest parish clergymen is secured. 3. That by this means a high standard of morality is maintained at the University. In all cases it would be meant that the good results are entirely due to the cause we are considering, or at least that they would be much diminished if the cause were to cease to operate.

Let us take the first head, and consider how far the restriction of the fellowships to clergymen preserves a succession of learned theologians. This an enquirer may determine for himself: let him ascertain how many works of permanent value in theology proceed from fellows of colleges. It is obvious to any person who is acquainted with the University that there are many most able and distinguished men who are in orders; but the ability and distinction relate to subjects which are unconnected with theology, and which would be as appropriate for a layman as for a clergyman. It is possible also to find persons who have really studied theology, and have gained a just reputation for their knowledge, but who give no obvious proof of it by the publication of books. This I think can hardly be considered a sufficient defence of the institution we are considering; the mere acquisition of knowledge which is never produced for the benefit of others can scarcely claim any special commendation.

There are indirect testimonies which seem to shew that the public display of theological attainments is but small. During the last two years a syndicate has been occupied in the University in the preparation of a scheme for theological examinations. An able critic on examining the programme thus drawn up made the remark that although the subjects chosen were very valuable in the way of preparation, yet of actual theology there was very little. The fact was that this defect had been repeatedly noticed during the deliberations of the syndicate; but every attempt to supply it had failed. In vain had it been suggested that there should be systematic treatises studied on such important subjects as Miracles, Prophecy, the Evidences of Religion, Christian Doctrine; the constant reply was that no suitable works existed. In fact some of the theological professors seemed really to hold that there was no such thing as theology; and a layman could not help thinking of Cicero's well-known wonder as to how

one soothsayer could look another in the face without
laughing. It certainly seemed both remarkable and
lamentable that the well-endowed University professorships, and the valuable cathedral preferment, had during
a long lapse of years according to the judgment of the
high authorities produced nothing that could be recommended for study in the most essential departments of
Christian Theology; so that students for the ministry
were to be left to ramble through the noxious deserts
of Church History without an object and without a
guide.

That in Cambridge itself there is but slender confidence in our own theological resources appeared incidentally some few years since when a gentleman offered
to endow a lectureship to be filled by a delegate from
the University of Harvard. The fear was loudly expressed that we should be exposed to unsound teaching
in morals and theology. Although on our side we had
truth and twenty doctors of divinity, yet it was appre-
hended that we might be vanquished by the casual
attack of an itinerant American.

It has indeed been sometimes stated as an excuse
for the absence of more theological fruit in the University that the time of the residents is much occupied
in work of various kinds connected with their official
functions. How far this excuse is valid could only be
settled by a careful examination of particulars; but it
is at least very obvious that there are various engross-
ing occupations of a purely secular character which
might well be discharged by laymen, so that clergymen would be at liberty to devote themselves to more
spiritual functions; such for example are the college

bursarships, and the University registrarship, which seem to be absolutely unconnected with theology. The office of a *tutor* of a college in the technical sense of the word has generally been held appropriate for a clergyman; the work though not decidedly clerical may be said to approximate to it. But for lecturing in such subjects as classics or mathematics it does not appear that ordination is at all necessary. Even the literary activity of clergymen is often directed into channels which seem quite unconnected with theology. Thus I have before me a list of nearly twenty works on conic sections which have been published by clergymen during the last few years, many of them fellows of colleges. It has been suggested that the pressure in this subject is owing to the idea of *infinity* which presents itself so conspicuously in discussing these curves, and which arrests the clerical attention.

Next we may consider how far the restrictions of some fellowships to persons in sacred orders secures for us a supply of laborious and zealous parish clergymen. This also is a matter which each person must decide for himself, and on which opinions will probably differ according to the circumstances under which observations have been made. There are cases in which a clerical fellow is engaged in laborious parochial work, and is partly supported by his fellowship; but these cases are not very numerous. Again it is said, and probably with great justice, that the incumbents of the college livings as a body are among the most respected of the clergy. There can be little doubt that in ability and discretion they take a very high position; and that these solid qualities may more than compensate for the want of any extravagant enthusiasm. But on the other hand it is asserted that the clerical fellows manifest great hesitation and reluctance in accepting the college livings; repeatedly it is found that a living is refused by one clerical fellow after another, so that those duties are shunned, for the performance of which it would seem that the clerical fellowships were instituted. Nor does Cambridge itself present a very prominent example of clerical activity. Collections have to be made annually for raising stipends for curates in some of the parishes; though it might perhaps have been anticipated that where so many appointments are practically secured to clergymen it would be possible to organise the clerical strength so as to supersede these appeals for charitable contributions.

Of course some of the objections urged under this head assume the soundness of those already considered under the first head. For instance it might be said that the disinclination to accept the college livings arises from the devotion to theological studies and teaching; but then the evidence of such devotion must be made manifest, and on this point to say the least there are grave suspicions.

There remains the topic of moral character and influence. It cannot be denied that there is some advantage apparently in the restriction of the fellowships to clergymen in this respect. The force of public opinion and the tone of society combine their aid to support clerical decorum. Tradition records cases in which laymen restricted to celibacy and indulged in idleness have disgraced themselves and their college. But then it must be remembered that instances of grave immorality on the part of clerical fellows, though happily rare, yet do occur. Moreover the more frequent spectacle of a clergyman who though not flagrantly vicious yet falls immeasurably below the meanest ideal of his sacred calling is scarcely less dangerous than the exhibition of open immorality. The young and uncorrupted student may we hope be repelled with disgust from any intimacy with those whose conduct is an obvious disgrace to their order; but it may be feared that the spectacle of men neither ignorant nor selfish, who are clerical only in name, must tend to bring the standard of excellence far below the point it might have reached under more elevating influences.

I have said nothing about one advantage which is sometimes supposed to follow from the restriction of the fellowships to clergymen, namely that by this means a quicker rate of succession is kept up as more vacancies are produced than would otherwise occur. It may be urged that the machinery set in operation is of far too serious a kind to justify its use for such an accidental purpose. Moreover it is obvious that if a rapid succession is desirable it may be attained by some regulation of uniform fairness, such as making all fellowships terminate after a fixed number of years. Certainly if one person is to be ejected from his fellowship because he has not taken orders, then it would scarcely be unjust to treat in the same way a person who has rejected say three college livings unless he had as a set-off produced some valuable theological work: for it would seem obvious that he could be little more than a nominal clergyman.

But I apprehend that the question as to clerical

fellowships may be considered practically decided; and
that the restriction cannot be much longer maintained.
The recent action of parliament has removed all religious tests which barred the admission to fellowships;
it has decided, for example, that young men of devout
character and eminent ability shall not be excluded
from fellowships merely because their father preached
the doctrines of Robert Hall with eloquence scarcely
inferior to his. It can hardly be doubted that the
principle thus recognised will be carried still farther,
and thus students who have gained fellowships without
subscribing to any theological formularies will not be
compelled to renounce them hereafter unless they become ministers of an assigned church. I shall not
stay to consider the question as to the right to make
an alteration in the constitution of corporations which
have received bequests on certain conditions; the question has been frequently discussed, and probably all has
been said on it that is of importance. I will only remark that it is not uncommon to find persons who
insist sternly on the continuity of the English Church
notwithstanding the apparent chasm of the reforma-
tion, and who thus maintain the present right of the
members of that church to benefactions left under very
different circumstances; as for example to funds intended to secure perpetual masses for the soul of the
founder. Then, granting the force of this principle, it
must be allowed that the character and extent of the
Church of England has been merely settled by parliament; and thus we may acquiesce if the boundaries
of that church are hereafter widely extended by the
same authority.

There seems now to be a growing feeling that clergymen should be such in reality, and not in appearance only; and in correspondence with this a desire to see secular duties discharged by laymen. During the last quarter of a century many professorships at the University have in natural course been vacated and filled up; and on the whole there is a steady tendency to choose laymen for all but the purely ecclesiastical appointments.

Probably if the clerical fellowships are retained there will be some change effected in the mode of appointment to the college livings. As we have already stated, living after living is declined by clerical fellows who have established no claim to be regarded as theologians, and who can therefore only be classed in the list of parish incumbents in order to justify their continued enjoyment of their fellowships. It was proposed by the University Commission to adopt a new scheme for the succession to the livings. According to this scheme all persons who had been fellows, but had vacated their position by resignation or by marriage, were to have their names retained on a roll, and if in orders were to have in their turn an option of a living. Another scheme might be suggested; that the offer of a living should be made in turn to every member of the college; but instead of starting, as at present, every living with the senior fellow, each living should start with the first fellow on the list who has not yet had an offer of one.

But leaving the matter of clerical fellowships let us proceed to consider what are the prominent defects which are said to be obvious in the University. My

T.   8

remarks will principally apply to mathematics, but
their range will by no means be confined to that
study.

If an undergraduate requires training for the Mathematical Tripos and will place himself in the hands of
one of the popular private tutors, his wants will be
abundantly supplied; but this teaching is very costly,
and is limited in its range by the prescriptions of the
mathematical examinations.   The colleges also have
staffs of mathematical lecturers, who supply the same
kind of training as the private tutors.   The college
lecturers, however, seem less appreciated than the
private tutors; one reason is that in the college
lecture rooms the students are not nearly so well
arranged and grouped as they are in the classes for
private instruction; and another reason may be that
the private tutor devotes himself more continuously to
his work, being occupied with it in the Long Vacation
as well as in Term time.

Of that public professional instruction which is often
regarded as the essence of a University, there is comparatively little in Cambridge.   During the last quarter
of a century out of the whole range of mixed mathematics lectures have been regularly delivered by professors
only on the following subjects : Optics, Hydrostatics,
Astronomical Instruments, and Lunar Theory.   I have
myself sometimes received letters of enquiry from
strangers who wished to study certain branches of pure
or mixed mathematics, and contemplated spending a
year or more at the University for the advantage of
professional lectures.   It was not quite satisfactory to be
compelled to reply that there was scarcely any of that

machinery for teaching of which the applicants seemed to assume the existence. It cannot be denied that there are serious difficulties : no professor can be expected to lecture to nearly empty benches, and except for examination purposes students can scarcely be induced to attend public instruction. The private tutors are naturally regarded as the safest guides to high places in the Tripos.

One favourite project of University Reformers is to convert fellows into teachers. A suitable provision is to be made for a teacher by giving him a double fellow-ship, or by some additional payment from the college funds, and he is then to supply instruction on nearly gratuitous terms. There are, however, grave difficulties to be encountered in such a scheme. It assumes that because a person has himself been ardent and successful in the pursuit of knowledge he will therefore be an able teacher, whereas experience shews that frequently this is not the case. A man may be highly susceptible of instruction who is not by any means apt to com-municate what he has received or acquired. Moreover, if the emoluments of the teacher are made very good, as is generally suggested, it is obvious that we remove all incentive to exertion in the special labour of instruc-tion. An idle man will prefer to rest on the stipend which is assured to him without any effort, rather than to undergo labour and trouble in order to augment that stipend to the amount of ten per cent. or fifteen per cent. And a person really interested in his subject will be tempted to give all his energy to the fascinating employment of original investigation rather than to the dull routine of elementary teaching.

The point seems to me of vital importance, for I have never seen any attempt to secure even the moderate performance of didactic functions after a good stipend has been assured. Sometimes in public discussion or private conversation a reference is made to the example of a distinguished teacher like the late Professor De Morgan, and it is hoped and assumed that we might have at Cambridge many such eminent masters in the science of instruction here. But I find that an important circumstance is generally overlooked, namely that the professorship which that remarkable man held was unendowed. Teaching with him was like private teaching in the University, so far as remuneration was involved; in kind at least, though not in degree. It may be said indeed that if the teachers were paid by endowment instead of by fee, we should obtain equally satisfactory results here; but this is an assertion which is perhaps at present inadequately supported by evidence. The mode of securing remuneration may be of the essence of the matter, and not a mere point of detail.

Indeed, whatever we may be fortunate enough to obtain in the future, it can hardly be said that our professorial staff at present is very much engaged in teaching. Many persons hold that such occupation is neither desirable nor necessary, and that it is sufficient if the professor resides and affords a salutary example, and is ready to answer any enquiry that may be addressed to him. An ardent reformer here came to the conclusion that no very definite function has been assigned to the professors, and that no very obvious duty was discharged by them; according to him the commission which they receive is "to adorn the University and meanwhile to lecture the poll men." The former function is somewhat indefinite, and the latter somewhat inglorious.

A phenomenon which has recently presented itself elsewhere deserves to be noticed: we find professors themselves asking for a release from all teaching duties. Thus a very eminent member of the class has stated that government ought to maintain in certain specified universities, besides professors of natural philosophy whose business should be to teach their subject, others who should be left quite free to pursue at their own discretion original research. The proposal has been pronounced by some critics bold, and by others audacious. It has been said that there is no ground on which the scheme can be limited to the subject of natural philosophy. In mathematics, chemistry, natural history, medicine, ancient and modern languages, civil history, law, and theology, it will be equally satisfactory to the professors to have their stipends secured and all the labour put out. But then the difficulty arises as to the mode in which the enormous expense is to be met, and still more as to the mode of dispensing the enormous patronage thus created. If an office involves substantial work there is some security that it will be worthily bestowed; but ornamental sinecures seem invariably to become the objects of jobbery and corruption. It is scarcely necessary to look beyond cathedral preferment to see that where there is pay and no work there is little security that the prizes will fall to the most deserving claimants. It is a common saying that it requires a century to eradicate the traces of the family of a single bishop from a diocese. And although it may be said that no grievous scandal arises if an appointment is filled by a tolerably respectable incumbent; yet the consequences of a perpetual disposal of valuable offices by mere interest or influence form a serious aggregate of corruption to public morality and of danger to general security. Moreover as to the suggestions we are considering, it has been remarked that when a race of ornamental professors has been appointed, and supplemented by the corresponding series of working teachers, the latter in their turn will supplicate for subordinates to whom they may hand over the work while retaining the emolument; and so on in a perpetual series.

As we have hinted above, the difficulty of finding a good method of electing to a professorship which is wholly or partially a sinecure, is one of the greatest practical obstacles to this mode of employing the resources of the University. Every scheme in use seems bad. The election by the University at large is tumultuous and capricious; but as an eminent resident of long experience has recently observed the election by Boards does not seem preferable.

If however appointments can be made with purity and judgment there seems nothing that can afford fairer promise of utility than to bestow upon men of proved ability and energy the means of devoting themselves to study with the view of advancing knowledge. The power which has been given to the colleges to confer fellowships on men of distinction in literature or science, without any regard to the restrictions of celibacy or sacred orders, seems to present many advantages. The college has ample means of forming a judgment as to the ability and industry of men who may seem to be worthy of such an advantage; and at the same time has a natural interest in connecting with its own institution the names of conspicuous men. A few fellowships have been conferred at Cambridge in accordance with the powers thus bestowed at the last revision of the college statutes; and perhaps there is some tendency to advance further in this direction.

In concluding this part of the essay it may be said that the schemes of some of our University reformers seem to want definiteness of aim and adequate provision of means. It is not sufficient to require only that an abundant shower of professors shall fall on the University like the shower of curates which a popular novelist tells us has fallen on the wild moors of the north; nor is it very practical to hope for a millennium of teaching in which two professors shall be found contending for every pupil. There must be distinct objects proposed; it must be settled whether the professor is to teach or merely to pursue private investigation; then if teaching is to be a prominent duty the machinery which will ensure due zeal and variety should be provided. If private investigation is to be the chief end of the institution some means must be devised to secure the necessary leisure undisturbed; the professors must be shielded from the incessant and importunate demands made on them to discharge the formal business of academical institutions and scientific societies; these occupations which are only indirectly and remotely connected with science absorb now far too much of the time and energy of the most eminent men. Finally stipends ought to be secured which shall be commensurate with the important duty to be discharged; and modes of appointment devised which will secure the selection of the worthiest candidate.

There are perhaps few matters on which the more earnest University Reformers are so bent as the conversion of the Headships of the Colleges into offices of more immediate literary or scientific significance. All admit that these offices are the most dignified in the University; and they are also the most lucrative, with the exception perhaps of that of cook in the largest college. Those who are dissatisfied with the present constitution affirm that the results obtained are not in proportion to the emoluments enjoyed; and it is customary to say that the duties of the Heads of Colleges are little more than nominal. If we consider only the work which is necessarily incumbent on the Heads of Colleges it may appear very slight; and there may be those in the list who are content to perform just this compulsory minimum. But on the other hand there is a very large amount of University business which has to be transacted; and in this some of the Heads of Colleges do spend much time and trouble. Whether this business could be transacted more ably and more economically may be a question for consideration; but there can be no doubt as to the fact that at present it falls to the share of the Heads of Colleges. The fairest way to regard the Heads of Colleges is not individually but as a body. Regarded individually it may be difficult to find adequate reason for the existence of the office. A Head of a College may if he please confine himself to such routine duty as occurs within his own college; and that this is but small in amount may be conjectured from the circumstance that owing to old age and infirmity there may be little direct action of a Head of a College during many years of his tenure of office. Indeed it is said that cases have occurred in which there could have been scarcely a nominal discharge of any duty. If we adopt the theory that the Heads of Colleges constitute a class to be mainly occupied in University business we see that in the ordinary course of events there will always be those who from comparative youth and vigour will be able to discharge the duties, even if some owing to great age or natural decay are no longer very efficient. If on the other hand the office of a Head of a College is considered to be important and significative mainly in reference to the college it would seem obvious that there must be need of a system by which a substitute or deputy could be appointed when the burden of the office became oppressive.

It does not appear that any adequate justification can be found for restricting the office to clergymen; whatever the duties may have been in former times, they do not seem at present to be specially clerical. In some colleges the master also acts as Bursar, which involves purely secular work. It has been said half seriously and half in joke that at the last revision of the statutes one large college would have abolished the clerical restrictions, but for the circumstance that the Master is there appointed by the Crown, and thus some insignificant court functionary might have obtained the dignity. It must be added that with the present restriction and mode of appointment that college has obtained a most illustrious succession of masters.

The fact that the Heads of Colleges are nearly all clergymen gives a curious significance to a grim remark made by the late well-known Charles Simeon. He had mentioned with great satisfaction some recent success of missionary labour in South Africa, and adds : "Alas, alas, it is easier to convert many Hottentots than a single Head of a College."

If the custom or the restriction which requires the Masters of Colleges to be clergymen were abrogated, it is conceivable that in some cases men of great scientific eminence could be found who would discharge the duties of the office creditably, and yet secure leisure for their own pursuits. We find it recorded in the life of Newton that some attempt was made to obtain for him the Provostship of King's College : it might be safely said that no greater honour could be conferred on any academical society.

As in the case of every office which combines dignity with emolument there is a difficulty in devising a good method of appointment. At present in every case of importance, except that in which the Crown has the right to present, the election is in the hands of the fellows of the college. It is easy to urge objections to this plan, but it is not so easy to suggest positive improvements. As long as the livings are offered in rotation to the fellows, beginning with the senior, it is obvious that seniority involves great advantages to clerical fellows ; thus an elector is naturally inclined to vote for a person above himself on the list rather than

for a person below himself. In the former case he will
gain a step if the candidate for whom he votes is
successful, but in the latter case he gains nothing.
This objection would be weakened by the adoption of
some such system as I suggested before for disposing
of the livings, by virtue of which every fellow would
receive one offer before any fellow received a second
offer. Or the right to vote at the election of a master
might be extended from the *actual* fellows, and made
to include all who had been fellows.

In discussions as to University Reform, when some
attempt has been made to shew that the duties of the
master of a college are very slight, the retort has been
sometimes made that the fellows have still fewer duties,
or in fact none at all. A story is told of a visitor
to one of our Universities who put himself under the
care of one of the self-constituted guides who obtrude
their services. Members of the various ranks of the
academical state were pointed out to the stranger—
heads of colleges, professors, and ordinary fellows; and
some attempt was made to describe the nature of the
functions discharged by the heads and professors. But
an inquiry as to the duties of fellows produced and
reproduced only the answer, "Them's fellows I say."
The guide had not been able to attach the notion of
even the pretence of duty to a fellowship.

It may be added that a vague notion does seem to
prevail that hereafter in the course of reform the fellows
will in some way teach something to somebody; but
nothing very definite has yet been suggested, with
perhaps one exception, which I will now notice. This
amounts to employing the fellows as literary and scien-

tific missionaries in various parts of England. I do not
see my way quite so clearly in this matter as many of
the able men by whom the scheme has been advocated.
I will not repeat the difficulty which has been already
implicitly noticed, namely, that fellows are chosen for
their skill and readiness in gaining knowledge, which
is by no means the same thing as imparting it to
others ; so that by merely directing and paying a man
to be an educational missionary we do not secure any
efficient discharge of the appropriate functions.   But I
will advert to another perplexity, namely, the choice of
suitable stations for the academical agents.   It would
be surely superfluous to attempt to supply such pecuniary aid as this scheme involves to places like Manchester, Liverpool, or Birmingham : for I suppose that
these wealthy towns, if they chose to put forth their
strength, could buy up the entire University and
colleges.   On the other hand, if the representative is
sent to some small place, too poor to pay for such an
instructor out of its own resources, there would probably
be scarcely any pupils to require his services.

It would be awkward if the missionary should find
himself inferior to some of the heathens whom he had
been appointed to elevate and transform.   As I write
I find that a distinguished resident at Manchester
points with just pride to Dalton and Joule, and asserts
that their scientific achievements surpass those of an
entire University ancient and well endowed.

It must be remembered that we have only a finite
supply of men to meet the demands which are made on
the University.   Much time and labour have to be
given to the necessary business of the place, and there

are moreover incessant applications to supply examiners on every subject at every place.

I will venture to give a few miscellaneous suggestions which will probably appear very timid and inefficient to an advanced reformer, though perhaps bold enough to offend the friends of the existing state of things.

The habit of looking on the fellowships as mere rewards for past industry and attainments, however unsatisfactory in theory, seems to be that which is practically adopted. If there is no prospect of changing this habit it would be, I think, a great improvement in detail to double the number of fellowships, reducing of course the emolument to half its present amount. In fact, owing to the improved condition of the property, the fellowships have much increased in value during the last twenty-five years, so that in some cases they are now nearly double what they were at the beginning of the period. If the competition was then severe enough, it would be so now if the value should be reduced to its former level. The advantage of increasing the number of the fellowships is that the area is thus much widened from which we may look for the science and learning of the future. Experience shews that of the seeds scattered a considerable fraction is wasted ; by supplying more seed we shall probably obtain a more plentiful harvest. I know it may be said that expenses have increased, so that a given nominal value represents less purchasing power now than it did formerly ; but I reply that the necessary expenses of the studious course in preparation for future usefulness have not appreciably advanced. A man may live in college engaged in his chosen literary or scientific pursuits as frugally now as a quarter of a century since: the presence of increased expense is felt only in connexion with unnecessary luxury of living at home, or with vagabondising over Europe for a fifth of the year. I hold then that if no change is to be made in the present theory as to the nature of a fellowship, much advantage would ensue from enlarging the number so as to offer to a larger class the assistance so welcome in the early stages of the serious pursuits of life.

The restrictions to celibacy and to sacred orders will probably not be long retained. To ensure a due supply of fellowships, if it be considered necessary to maintain the principle of using them as rewards, they might be made tenable for a fixed period, say ten years. It may, however, be said with great justice that experiments are now in fact being carried on, and the results may be watched before any further steps are taken. For instance in some of the colleges the restriction to celibacy has been removed, and thus fellowships are held by married men. If, as may naturally be expected, these colleges, by thus retaining and paying some of their ablest men, obtain a position in the University and the country more than commensurate with their relative numbers and resources, it will be a significant hint to the colleges which at present keep to the old system to adopt the new course. But if the presence of a decided proportion of married fellows in a college does not produce the valuable results which have been anticipated, the advantage of the change becomes questionable.

Perhaps something might be done to develop the

principle of giving fellowships occasionally, not for mere examination triumphs in youth, but for mature labour in literature or science. It has been suggested that a certain number of fellowships, say one in eight or ten, should be employed in this way; the election to them might be left to the colleges, subject to the approval of some general board. At present it can hardly be doubted that fellowships are occasionally apparently wasted. In some years by accident there may be a large number of vacancies, and thus a candidate may be fortunate who has failed on former occasions, and would have no chance had it not been for the favourable opportunity. Thus a person may obtain a fellowship whose character and power are well known by an experience of six or seven years, and who, although possessing respectable attainments, gives no promise of ever rising above mediocrity. Much would be gained if the fellowship, instead of being conferred on a person who will never illustrate the college, could be used as the means of securing the leisure of one whose past career abundantly demonstrated that his leisure would be most beneficially employed. The world it has been said forms a court of revision for conferring or annulling the judgments of academical examiners; and it would be well if the revised decisions could carry with them some reasonable emolument.

The practice of examining candidates for fellowships, still retained in the two large colleges, seems very unsatisfactory. The subjects are in general the same as those of the principal university examinations, and it is unlikely that the staff of a single college will supply better examiners than the whole University.

The effect of the practice is to retain men working at examination subjects when they ought to be engaged in more important business, and moreover the result may frequently be to secure the reward not to the ablest but to the richest. The fortunate man whose circumstances enable him to prolong his training for examinations has an enormous advantage over a poorer candidate who must begin to work for his living. It is sometimes said that by these college examinations a candidate who has been unlucky in the University examinations has an opportunity of repairing his misfortune; the answer is that the candidate has been during his undergraduate course repeatedly examined in college, and thus ample means already exist for a judgment on his relative attainments.

There are various other subjects which are so connected with the Universities that it is necessary at least to allude to them in any essay like the present. One of them is the state of education in the large public schools. How important this matter is may be seen from the statement of the late Dr Whewell, that those who wish to improve English education ought to direct their attention to the schools rather than to the Universities. See his work *Of a Liberal Education in General, &c.*, Art. 363, reproduced in the *Report of the Public Schools Commission*, Vol. II., page 45. That a youth, after a long course at school and at the University, may remain with little knowledge and little mental training is too painfully certain. There may be some doubts as to where the blame principally lies, but at least it may be said that in schools there is more power of control than in the University, and so more ought to be accomplished with unwilling pupils. Perhaps if the University could be induced to establish a good matriculation examination, the schools would be stimulated to increased exertion. Something ought to be done to discourage the existence of a class of persons popularly called *poll-tutors*, a class the existence of which has been pronounced by a most distinguished scholar a "nearly unmixed evil." The function of these tutors is to prepare the inferior students for the ordinary examinations. Tales which are current as to the nature of the process are probably fictions or gross exaggerations, but they perhaps indicate some of the tendencies of the system. Thus it has been reported that instruction has been sometimes conveyed to a class supplied with beer and tobacco ; and it has been hinted that the facts of Scripture History and the elements of theology have been woven into doggrel verse for the benefit of weak memories. The University is to blame if it admits to its privileges the idle youths for whom these appliances are necessary. It may be safely said that with moderate ability and application the college instruction is adequate for the ordinary examinations.

It may be that the Universities themselves are to blame for the tendency observable in schools to give an undue share of attention to the most forward pupils. The prizes of scholarships and fellowships are so conspicuous that the habit has long existed of working as it were for them, and of measuring the reputation of a school by the success of its picked boys, rather than by the average attainments of the whole. The system of minor scholarships established during the last few years in the University, and the local examinations, have

T.   9

probably strengthened the habit. Thus, generally
speaking, we have in a school large classes composed of
the younger and backward boys, and small classes of
the older and more advanced ; the smaller classes also
being committed to the more mature and able teachers.
See the *Report of the Public Schools Commission,* Vol. II.,
pages 16 and 17; where the subject is noticed by Mr.
Riddell under section 1 of his letter, and by Mr.
Hedley under section 9.

The Public School Commissioners, with sound judgment, wished to examine the schools in order to form
an opinion of the results obtained with respect to boys
of average industry and capacity ; and it is a most
significant fact that the head-masters declined to assent
to the proposition. See the *Report of the Public Schools
Commission,* Vol II., pages 6 to 9.

The vacations at schools are considered by many
persons to be unreasonably long ; it may be said that
the labours of teachers in schools are very wearisome,
and that numerous and considerable seasons of relaxation are indispensable. But it may be replied that the
duty cannot be so severe as that of physicians, lawyers,
and clergymen, who are compelled to be content with
much rarer and shorter vacations. Nor do I think that
the pressure on a master in a school is so severe as that
which is borne by an active private tutor at the University. Some years since, when public and private
lectures in one of the large colleges had already been
resumed after the Christmas vacation, a fellow of the
college, who was also a master in a well-known school,
appeared in the hall, and to the enquiry which was
made as to when his duty would commence he vaguely

indicated some day in the ensuing week; it was suggested to him that as Easter fell very early in that year it was scarcely necessary to take the trouble of reassembling the school until after that epoch.

The excessive cultivation of athletic sports is characteristic both of schools and Universities; and it would be desirable by some conjoint effort to check this extravagance. It may be said that amusements are essential; but the just complaint is against the absorbing interest taken in these pastimes. Public and private tutors must too often be conscious that even if the bodies of the pupils are delivered with reasonable regularity to the lecture-rooms, the thought and interest are still on the river or in the cricket-ground; a student once almost drove a lecturer frantic by pleading as an excuse for absence from instruction, what he called "attendance to his boating *duties.*" There are many men in the University whose sole occupation seems to be *rowing;* it is difficult to form a conception of the mission of this class of students; sometimes one might fancy they were intended for the lake-dwellers invented or discovered by modern science, but displaced by some accident through a few thousand years. It would not be prudent to institute any enquiry as to the disposal of these watermen after they leave the University, for fear of the discovery that they mostly reappear as clergymen.

It can hardly be doubted that in the course of a few years we shall see some great changes made in the employment and distribution of the revenues of the Colleges and Universities. The annual income of half a million of money which may be the aggre-

gate of the revenues of Oxford and Cambridge is too
large to remain in these days without jealous scrutiny. It will probably not be considered an adequate
return for this vast revenue to furnish a fair supply of
lawyers, physicians and clergymen. For law and
physic are themselves lucrative professions, which
bring with them their own abundant reward ; and even
divinity offers dignity and emolument as the temporal
accidents of spiritual things ; not to mention the large
ecclesiastical patronage of the colleges themselves. It
would seem that the revenues instead of offering superfluous prizes for well-remunerated professions ought to
be devoted nearly exclusively to the advancement and
diffusion of learning and science. There are some persons who seriously doubt the advantage of all endowments; and certainly we need not go far to find very
discouraging cases of the failure of ample bequests to
secure the benefits proposed. Thus for example, in
spite of the vast estate which is available for education
at Bedford, subscriptions have been sought for erecting
a county school; though the endowment ought to suffice
amply for all the education required. So also a project
has been started for a county school in Cambridge,
where it might be supposed that some of the ample
college resources could be expended for this end.

By a proper and economical employment of the
University and College funds it might be possible to
avoid the perpetual appeals to government for assistance in scientific objects. I am well aware that it is
the popular fashion to demand large sums from the ministry of the day for the prosecution of any scheme
that may be taken up by busy enthusiasts; but I

cannot help recording my dislike to the system. I conceive that when any such application has been made the expense should be estimated, and then the question should be carefully discussed whether the proposed operation is really that to which the computed amount can be most profitably applied, or whether any other object has superior claims. As it is, the most pertinacious applicants now secure the aid of government, without any discriminating enquiry as to whether they are also the most deserving.

I may probably carry few of my readers with me in two suggestions which I will venture to propose.

One is that it would be well if the University ceased to return members to Parliament. If the constituency resided at the University there might be some reason perhaps for this privilege; but the mass of voters scattered over the country principally consisting of men who have taken an ordinary degree, does not compose any such aggregate of learning and science as to deserve any special representation. For many years past moreover the members of Parliament for the University, however estimable, have rarely been persons of great academical distinction, or specially qualified to speak on such subjects as may be supposed to affect academical institutions.

The other point is the constitution of the *Electoral Roll*, that is of the body of residents who have reached the degree of M.A. and to whom important privileges are confided. It seems to me that merely the possession of an ordinary degree ought not to bring with it this honour and duty; and therefore I should like to see the list confined to those who are or had been

fellows of colleges, or who had held certain specified
University offices, such as those of examiners. It is
obvious that some such qualification is necessary to ensure creditable attainments in the members of the Roll.

But to return to the University : as I have said, we
may confidently expect considerable changes soon ; that
the proposal of them will be met by stout resistance
may also be expected, but judging from past experience
when once reforms are made by external authority
acquiescence readily follows. As on former occasions
we may have sensational pamphlets with the indignant
motto : *If the foundations be destroyed, what can the
righteous do?:* and we shall probably again see that
the righteous arrange comfortable dwellings for themselves out of the fragments. That the natural sciences
will gain largely by the changes may also be anticipated ; for both from without and from within the
claims of these subjects are vigorously urged. Some
among ourselves seem, perhaps with a little inconsistency,
to advocate the encouragement of natural history, while
yet they uphold the restriction of the fellowships to
clergymen ; as I have already remarked, we may naturally look upon theology as the principal if not the exclusive pursuit of those in sacred orders.

Important as natural history, and especially physiology may be, I venture to wish rather than to hope
that the older studies which relate to the *mind* may
retain that supremacy which seems rightly to belong to
them in comparison with all that relates to the struc-
ture of men and animals. A very distinguished scholar
has startled us lately by recording the fear that the
knowledge of Greek can hardly be expected to maintain

its present level in England ; many persons will receive this expression of opinion, from a calm well-qualified judge, with the pain which results from the conviction that it is sound, and that the principle may be extended further. A decline in the state of Greek scholarship implies even more than the failure of esteem for the most valuable and influential of all languages ; it involves with it a gradual but certain decay of general culture, the sacrifice of learning to science, the neglect of the history of man and of thought for the sake of facts relating to the external world.

No one who has resided long at the University can avoid expressing the hope that whatever changes may await us, the great merits which belong to the place will remain unimpaired. We may be sanguine enough to believe that here especially the keenest rivalry of youthful contests may be accompanied with generous appreciation of a competitor's merits and may often issue in the sincerest friendship, that the richest stores of learning are freely placed by those who have gained them at the disposal of enquirers, and that respect and esteem are readily accorded to the claims of ability and character. It is interesting to read the testimony which the late Mr. Hopkins bore from his long experience to the merit of the pupils who had come under his notice ; see page 249 of the *Evidence* attached to the *Report of the Cambridge University Commission.*

ELEMENTARY GEOMETRY.

IT has been said by a distinguished philosopher that England is "usually the last to enter into the general movement of the European mind." The author of the remark probably meant to assert that a man or a system may have become famous on the continent, while we are almost ignorant of the name of the man and the claims of his system. Perhaps, however, a wider range might be given to the assertion. An exploded theory or a disadvantageous practice, like a rebel or a patriot in distress, seeks refuge on our shores to spend its last days in comfort if not in splendour. Just when those who originally set up an idol begin to suspect that they have been too extravagant in their devotions we receive the discredited image and commence our adorations. It is a less usual but more dangerous illustration of the principle, if just as foreigners are learning to admire one of our peculiarities we should grow weary of it.

In teaching elementary geometry in England we have for a long time been accustomed to use the well-known *Elements of Euclid*. At the present moment, when we learn from the best testimony, namely, the admission of anti-Euclideans, that both in France and Italy dissatisfaction is felt with the system hitherto used, accompanied with more or less desire to adopt ours, we are urged by many persons to exchange our system for one which is falling out of favour on the continent.

Various incidental parts of the subject will be discussed in the present essay, more especially those which appear to have been overlooked; and it is hoped that there will be no transgression of the limits of courtesy in the criticisms offered on any opinions which may be quoted.

Many assertions have been made in discussion which rest entirely on the authority of the individual advocate, and thus it is necessary to be somewhat critical in our estimate of the value of the testimony. Two witnesses who are put prominently forward are MM. Demogeot and Montucci, who drew up a report on English education for the French Government. Now I have no doubt that these gentlemen were suited in some respects to report on English education, as they were selected for that purpose; but I have searched in vain for any evidence of their special mathematical qualifications. No list of mathematical publications that I have consulted has ever presented either of these names, and I am totally at a loss to conceive on what grounds an extravagant respect has been claimed for their opinions. The following sentence has been quoted with approbation from these writers: "Le trait distinctif de l'enseignement des mathématiques en Angleterre c'est qu'on y fait appel plutôt à la mémoire qu' à l'intelligence de l'élève." In the first place we ought to know on what evidence this wide generalisation is constructed. Did the writers visit some of the humbler schools in England in which the elements of arithmetic and mensuration were rudely taught, and draw from this narrow experience an inference as to the range of mathematical instruction throughout England? Or did they find on inspecting some of our larger public schools that the mathematical condition was unsatisfactory? In the latter case this might have arisen from exclusive devotion to classics, or from preference for some of the fashionable novelties of the day, or from want of attention and patience in the teachers. On the most unfavourable supposition the condemnation pronounced on the general mathematical training in England cannot be justified. But take some kind of experimental test. Let an inquirer carefully collect the mathematical examination papers issued throughout England in a single year, including those proposed at the Universities and the Colleges, and those set at the Military Examinations, the Civil Service Examinations, and the so-called Local Examinations. I say then, without fear of contradiction, that the original problems and examples contained in these papers will for interest, variety, and ingenuity surpass any similar set that could be found in any country of the world. Then any person practically conversant with teaching and examining can judge whether the teaching is likely to be the worst where the examining is the most excellent.

The sentence quoted from MM. Demogeot and Montucci, in order to have any value, ought to have proceeded from writers more nearly on a level with the distinguished mathematical teachers in England. So far as any foundation can be assigned for this statement, it will probably apply not to mathematics especially but to all our studies, and amount to this, that our incessant examinations lead to an over cultivation of the memory. Then as to the practical bearing of the remark on our present subject it is obvious that the charge, if true, is quite independent of the textbook used for instruction, and might remain equally valid if Euclid were exchanged for any modern author.

The French gentlemen further on contrast what they call Euclid's verbiage with the elegant conciseness of the French methods. It is surely more than an answer to these writers to oppose the high opinion of the merits of Euclid expressed by mathematicians of European fame like Duhamel and Hoüel. See the *First Report of the Association for the Improvement of Geometrical Teaching*, page 10.

When we compare the lustre of the mathematical reputation of these latter names with the obscurity of the two former, it seems that there is a great want of accuracy in the statement made in a recent circular : "The opinion of French mathematicians on this question, is plainly expressed in the Report of MM. Demogeot and Montucci...."

I should have to quote very largely indeed if I wished to draw attention to every hazardous statement which has been advanced; I must therefore severely restrain myself. Consider the following : "Unquestionably the best teachers depart largely from his words, and even from his methods. That is, they use the work of Euclid, but they would teach better without it. And this is especially true of the application to problems. Everybody recollects, even if he have not the daily experience, how unavailable for problems

a boy's knowledge of Euclid generally is." The value
of such a statement depends entirely on the range of
the experience from which it has been derived. Suppose for instance that the writer had been for many
years an examiner in a large University in which
against each candidate's name the school was recorded
from which he came; suppose that the writer had also
been much engaged in the numerous examinations connected with the military institutions; suppose that
he had also been for a quarter of a century in residence
at one of the largest colleges at Cambridge, and actively
employed in the tuition; suppose also that it had been
his duty to classify the new students for lecture purposes by examining them in Euclid and other parts
of elementary mathematics; and finally suppose that
he was in constant communication with the teachers
in many of the large schools: then his opinion would
have enjoyed an authority which in the absence of
these circumstances cannot be claimed for it.

If I may venture to refer to my own experience,
which I fear commenced when the writer whom I have
just quoted was in his cradle, I may say that I have
taught geometry both Euclidean and non-Euclidean,
that my own early studies and prepossessions were
towards the latter, but that my testimony would now
be entirely in favour of the former.

Those who have been much engaged in private and
public teaching at the Universities know well which
schools send them the best students in any particular
branch of knowledge; some schools are really eminent,
others are conspicuous for their failure. Occasionally,
two schools are so nearly balanced in point of numbers

that it is almost impossible to avoid contrasting the academical fortunes of their pupils : such a comparison would be unsuitable for publication, but might be obtained privately from not a few well-qualified observers. Indeed it has sometimes occurred to me that those engaged in school teaching would gain much advantage if they endeavoured to ascertain what impression their pupils made, in comparison with others, on the resident members of the University with whom they came in contact. One college lecturer in mathematics used to say that he could detect the youths from a particular school almost as soon as they entered his class-room by their apparent firm belief in the equality of all mankind. The lecturer would propose a few examples for exercise ; then passing through the room he would glance at the solutions in progress. Here he would suggest to one, admitted to be a possible future senior wrangler, that the result obtained seemed unsatisfactory ; and the student would immediately commence a revision. Then passing to another, the lecturer would make a similar just suggestion ; and receive the answer almost immediately : "If you please, Sir, it is quite right." There was nothing in the tone of the remark which was objectionable, for there was no want of courtesy or respect; but in the opinion of the lecturer there was a grievous absence of the power of estimating comparative attainments. The youth was apparently unconscious of the incomparably superior knowledge of the lecturer, who had given almost as many mature years, as he had himself boyish weeks, to the study of mathematics.

But to return to our immediate subject. I admit

that to teach Euclid requires patience both from the tutor and the pupil; but I can affirm that I have known many teachers who have succeeded admirably, and have sent a large number of pupils to the University well skilled in solving deductions and examples; nor have I ever known a really able and zealous teacher to fail. I am happy to supplement my own testimony by an extract from the very interesting lecture on Geometrical Teaching by Dr Lees, of St Andrews. "Whatever may be the cause of failure in England, it is clear as any demonstration can be that the failure cannot be ascribed to Euclid. Because in Scotland we do employ Euclid as the text-book for our students, and in Scotland we have the teaching of Geometry attended with the most complete success; and this not only in the colleges, but in all the higher and more important schools and academies of the country, and in many of the parish schools even, where the attention of the teacher is necessarily so much divided." See also the remarkable *Narrative-Essay on a Liberal Education*, by the Rev. S. Hawtrey, A.M., Assistant-Master, Eton.

Some of the statements which have been made to the disadvantage of Euclid and his admirers seem to me extravagant enough to discredit the ablest advocate and endanger the soundest cause: in reading them it is necessary for the sake of fairness to remember the remark made by a judge after hearing a very injudicious speech from a barrister; that the jury must not punish the suitor on account of the indiscreet zeal of his counsel. Let me give a specimen from a preface published nearly forty years since: "And where, may I ask, can we find scaffolding more intricate, and apparatus more complicated, than those which Euclid has used in the erection of his geometrical temple ? Much valuable time will be saved to the student, when Euclid's Elements are consulted only by the antiquarian....But the syllogism has been already discarded as an incumbrance ; and it is to be hoped, that synthetical geometry will speedily share the same fate."

This reformer was in advance of his age, and indeed, judging from the last words of the extract, in advance even of the present age.

The following passage I find quoted in an article by an able cultivator and teacher of mathematics in the Quarterly Journal of Education for October, 1871 ; it is stated to be from an address delivered at Edinburgh. " From the majority of the papers in our few mathematical journals, one would almost be led to fancy that British mathematicians have too much pride to use a simple method, while an unnecessarily complex one can be had. No more telling example of this could be wished for than the insane delusion under which they permit ' Euclid ' to be employed in our elementary teaching. They seem voluntarily to weight alike themselves and their pupils for the race." The British mathematical journals with the titles of which I am acquainted are the Quarterly Journal of Mathematics, the Mathematical Messenger, and the Philosophical Magazine ; to which may be added the Proceedings of the Royal Society and the Monthly Notices of the Astronomical Society. I should have thought it would have been an adequate employment, for a person engaged in teaching, to read and master these periodicals regularly ; but that a single mathematician should be able to improve more than half the matter which is thus presented to him fills me with amazement. I take down some of these volumes, and turning over the pages I find article after article by Professors Cayley, Salmon, and Sylvester —not to mention many other highly distinguished names. The idea of amending the elaborate essays of these eminent mathematicians seems to me something like the audacity recorded in poetry with which a superhuman hero climbs to the summit of the Indian Olympus and overturns the thrones of Vishnu, Brahma, and Siva. While we may regret that such ability should be exerted on the revolutionary side of the question there is at least one mournful satisfaction ; the weapon with which Euclid is assailed was forged by Euclid himself. The justly celebrated professor, from whose address the quotation is taken, was himself trained by those exercises which he now considers worthless : twenty years ago his solutions of mathematical problems were rich with the fragrance of the Greek geometry. I venture to predict that we shall have to wait some time before a pupil will issue from the reformed school, who singlehanded will be able to challenge more than half the mathematicians of England.

But let me notice the absence of connexion between the two parts of the passage ; although the latter is said to be a *telling example* of the former. I pass by the words *insane delusion* with just an expression of regret at the attempt to make uncomplimentary epithets stand in the vacancy caused by the absence of arguments ; and I observe that it is difficult to see how the study of Euclid can lead to the bad choice of methods by our great mathematicians in their memoirs. Elementary geometry rarely occurs in these abstruse investigations; and when it does occur there is no compulsion to adopt Euclid's methods. A teacher may at the commencement of a study exercise his pupils with a minuteness and repetition, which will be laid aside as the pupils advance. Logical analysis and grammatical analysis may be taught and practised with stringency as an early exercise; and yet an accomplished speaker or writer may find after a time that the habits which he has acquired supersede the necessity of a continual recurrence to the elementary discipline. Similarly a youth may be advantageously trained in the rigorous methods of Euclid; and yet when in mature life he is speculating on ideal secants and circles at infinity he may be quite emancipated from his early restrictions.

Let me however meet a possible remark, or rather one that has been actually made, to the effect that the objections to Euclid are maintained by "a large number of the leading mathematical teachers in the best schools of the country." In the first place it must be observed that from the nature of things the amount of comparative dissatisfaction with any existing institution is often much exaggerated, because those who are satisfied with it do not publicly come forward to defend it. Some years since the scheme of mathematical instruction at Cambridge was undergoing revision by a large board composed of the most eminent professors and private teachers in the place. A letter was on one occasion noticed which had been addressed to the Board by a teacher in a school, who was probably younger than the youngest member present; the letter was anti-Euclidean and contained various formulæ of this kind : *the best teachers do so and so.* The members of the board indicated by unanimous silence as significantly as they could have done by the loudest testifying that they considered themselves as competent to judge of the best teaching as the writer ; and that their opinion was contrary to his. More recently a request has been courteously addressed to our Mathematical Board to allow substitutes for Euclid, and again unanimously declined.

In the next place let me notice that there is an ambiguity in the words *best schools.* If by *best* is meant largest and socially most esteemed, the answer is that a school may be eminent on various grounds, but far from eminent in mathematics. The weight to be attached to the opinion of the *leading mathematical teachers* must be measured by the distinction gained by their pupils. Thus for example the testimony of such a man as the late Professor De Morgan, remarkable for the success which attended his teaching, is of conspicuous value on this account. We must remember that this testimony is very different from the opinion of a person who has never been a teacher, or whose teaching has related to the experimental sciences rather than to mathematics.

Let me now pass to another matter suggested by the following words which I quote from a certain preface immediately after an appeal to MM. Demogeot and Montucci : "And unquestionably one result of the tediousness of Euclid is that so little knowledge of geometry is gained ; so little, there is abundant evidence to prove, that our education is more marked by inferiority to other nations in this respect than any other."

I say nothing at present with respect to the tedious-ness of Euclid; but I wish to consider the point as to which we are told there is abundant evidence, which however is not cited, namely our inferiority to other nations. The opinion of MM. Demogeot and Montucci cannot I think be accepted as decisive, because we have no adequate guarantee of their special qualifications for pronouncing a judgment. Reference is sometimes made to a Report on Foreign Education drawn up by a most distinguished English writer; but we must remember that the undisputed literary eminence of this person does not warrant us in attaching great weight to his opinion on mathematical proficiency, and indeed he himself candidly admits that he is not familiar with the subject.

This question of comparison is important; I am induced to think with an eminent politician that our ostentatious depreciation of ourselves in comparison with foreign countries is not creditable to us. But let us proceed to particulars, and examine the justice of what may be called the *argument of alarm* so far as relates to our science.

It is not obvious on what principle the comparison between ourselves and foreigners has been instituted by those who have pronounced a confident verdict against us. It would be manifestly inconclusive if an examiner were to take an English school at random and a foreign school at random, and compare the mathematical attainments of a class in the one school with those of a class of about the same age in the other school. Let us assume in the first place that the examiner is competent from his own knowledge of mathematics to form a trustworthy judgment on the subjects—a condition not always satisfied—still there are so many circumstances to be regarded that an accurate conclusion is by no means easy to obtain. It will be necessary to compare the amount of time given in the two schools to the study, and the credit which is attached to proficiency. It is obvious that in the large public schools of England the head-master is invariably a distinguished scholar, and the main energy of the pupils is directed to the ancient classics, mathematical studies occupying only a subordinate position. Further it is very important to ascertain if the school chosen at random is a good average specimen; I cannot say whether there is tolerable uniformity abroad, but in England there is frequently an immense difference between one school and another in this respect. I should regret very much to have the mathematical efficiency of elementary teaching in England estimated by some schools, and should abide with confidence a verdict formed on other schools.

Perhaps however an appeal is made not so much to the operations carried on in our schools, as to the general position of England in the knowledge of mathematics. There can be no doubt that the latter reference is often explicitly made or implicitly suggested. We are told in so many words that we ought to be abashed at our hopeless deficiency, and that we must abandon the insane delusions in which we indulge, so that we may be less shamefully distanced by our continental rivals.   At the risk of being tedious I shall discuss this point.

It is preposterous to suppose that England is to be matched with *all the continent;* but this is the notion which some people seem to entertain.   The German nation is far more numerous than ours; so also is the French; to say nothing of Italians and Russians. Thus so far is it from being just to compare England with all the continent that it is even unjust to compare it in respect to population with France, or Germany, or Russia singly.

But further.   In England the appointments open to scientific persons are utterly insignificant in number and importance ; for as I have said the head-masterships in the large public schools are invariably given to classical scholars.   Compare the few professorships in our Universities with the much larger number in Germany, and with the position which the French Institute offers to men of science.

Then again, look at our religious difficulties.   Up to the date at which I began to write these pages, a fellowship at the University could not be held by any Nonconformist or Romanist.   The practical result may be stated thus : the population of the empire naturally available for supplying the highest scientific development was reduced to about half of its nominal total. Further I may remark that after excluding half the population by tests, a further restriction was imposed by the custom or the regulation of requiring the holders of various desirable appointments to be clergymen.

I am not now expressing any opinion as to the

advantage or disadvantage attending such a national institution as the French Academy of Sciences, or as to the propriety of the abolition of all tests and restrictions at the University. I only wish to draw attention to the circumstances which influence the comparison I have in view; I need scarcely observe that religious opinions are no obstacle to the attainment of academical positions in foreign countries.

In the lapse of years it may happen that considerable changes will be produced in England, but when we are considering the present state of science in the country, we must consider the operation of the causes which have hitherto acted. It would I think be hardly too much to say that by the various impediments which have obstructed the free access to academic emoluments the available population from which we draw the cultivation of the highest departments of science has been reduced to about one-fourth of its nominal total. I have then I hope carried my readers with me in my argument to the conclusion that we should not be disgraced if our contributions to the advancement of mathematics reached even a fifth part of those of France, or a still smaller fraction of those of Germany.

I now leave the path of argument and take to that of opinion. My belief is that in the number and excellence of our eminent mathematicians, instead of reaching to only one-fifth of the standard of France we are on an equality. I do not arrogate to myself the power of judicially estimating the attainments and the productions of the greatest scientific men in two countries—if any person could claim that power it would doubtless be some professor whose

ample leisure and assured position gave him the opportunity for long and intense study. I can only form an
opinion from such surveys of the domain of science as
my scanty leisure has permitted; and perhaps a taste
for the history of mathematics has led me more naturally than others to the consideration of relative merit.
Let any person who doubts about the matter make
some such comparison as the following : let him choose
say the six men in France who are most eminent in
pure mathematics, and the six who are most eminent
in mixed mathematics; and then let him try if he
cannot write against each French name that of one
of our own countrymen of at least equal distinction.
Then let him extend the comparison so as to bring
in the names of men inferior to those of the highest
class. The trial is not difficult to make. French
mathematical works are published almost entirely by
one well-known firm, and by procuring a catalogue
from this firm the authors of distinct works can easily
be ascertained, while a list of the members of the Academy of Sciences will supply the names of those who
may have written important memoirs, but not distinct
works. I have sometimes amused myself by institu-
ting such a comparison as I have suggested; and thus
it is that I have gained some confidence as to the result.

Even so far as elementary works are concerned, we
have I think, little to fear from comparison; some of
our best productions have been translated into French :
others have been translated into Italian, which is
noteworthy since French mathematical literature would
in this case have furnished an easier resource and a
wider choice.

I have spoken of a comparison with France merely because the trial can be so easily made by any person who is interested in the subject; and because I think France has been more especially singled out for praise by those who have condemned our own training and its results. But I do not shun a comparison even with Germany; though, as I have said, we should not be disgraced if in amount we fell even below a fifth. Let the names of a dozen of the foremost German mathematicians be written down, and try to put some English name of equivalent eminence against each: there would I believe be but few blank places.

I remember being present a short time since at a party in Cambridge which had been collected to meet a visitor whose position at the head of English science would hardly be disputed. In the course of conversation he was asked whom he considered the most eminent of the foreign cultivators of mixed mathematics; the inquirer I fear half assuming that such a person must be much superior to any whom we could produce. The answer after some hesitation was to this effect: "It would be difficult to say, but I am confident that .... is a match for any of them." Few Cambridge men will have any difficulty in supplying the name of their own professor which I have left blank in the answer.

I venture then to maintain not as a paradox but as a sober truth that the mathematical reputation of England is second to that of no other nation; and that our position so far from casting any suspicion on the soundness of our system of elementary instruction does really strongly recommend that system.

I will not delay on a kindred topic, but I may remark that just as our English mathematical education is sometimes condemned from its assumed inferiority in results to that of France or Germany—an inferiority which seems altogether imaginary—so Cambridge itself has been sometimes reproached for its errors as demonstrated by an assumed inferiority to this or that University or College which has been more eager for innovations in methods and subjects of study. The answer which has been offered to such disparagement when expressed in conversation or debate consists in naming three or four of our most eminent men, each of whom has done singly more for science than the entire academic staff of the institution offered for comparison.

In speaking of English mathematicians it would be unpardonable to omit all reference to a phenomenon which is peculiar to this country; I mean the existence of an able and enthusiastic band of non-academical students. I do not assert that Euclid has been the sole geometrical guide of this distinguished body, but I may assert that he has been their principal guide, and has contributed mainly to their success : their writings exhibit the predominant influence of the Greek geometry. From this band of determined students arose Thomas Simpson, one of the greatest of English mathematicians ; and the succession of eminent names has been well kept up to our own day, and is still most honourably represented. It is much to be wished that the history of this remarkable cultivation of science should be collected and published; one gentleman has shewn by numerous able and interesting sketches of detached periods how competent he is to treat the whole, and I trust he will undertake the grateful task.

I am anxious to draw attention to the high position of England in mathematics, because as I have said this establishes the value of the elementary training which was employed in the education of our greatest representatives. I am surprised to find it asserted in a recent circular that Euclid "is an unsuitable preparation...for the higher mathematical training...of the present day." No reference is added to support this statement, so that it is not obvious on whose authority or experience it is based. Teachers much occupied with the "higher mathematical training" cannot be very numerous in England; and if we learned the names of those who have been unfortunate in their pupils owing to the use of Euclid we might be able to explain the causes of their failure. However as I have said the present state of mathematics in England shews that Euclid is *not* unsuitable to the purpose for which it is used; and the testimony of the eminent teachers in Cambridge, which must surely outweigh that of the comparatively small number occupied in the higher mathematical training elsewhere, is decidedly of the same character.

I will not lay stress on a point to which I will advert; namely that both in the construction and solution of problems the superiority of English, and especially of Cambridge mathematicians, is I apprehend indisputable and undisputed. One of the French mathematical journals devotes great space to problems and their solution; and it seems to me that for ingenuity and elegance both fall far below our own. I do not however wish to press the consideration, for I do not consider the invention of problems as the most important application of mathematical ability; but at least it may serve to repel the charge brought against our elementary geometry that it is marked by *unsuggestiveness*; and perhaps the same kind of objection is intended to be conveyed by the statement that " Euclid has been fossilized by age."

It has been urged by a determined opponent of Euclid that the relative merits of various systems of geometry should be tested by experiments; he says : " The main question, as to whether Euclid should be retained or not, would be more satisfactorily settled by an accurate induction from a sufficient number of carefully worked experiments, than by any number of theoretical arguments, or *a priori* considerations. Though we make this remark, as if the question were an open one, we have no manner of doubt as to the conclusion to which an impartial and thorough investigation would lead."

The confidence thus expressed in the anti-Euclidean side of the contest could be asserted with as much emphasis on the other side by persons of equal mathematical reputation with the author whom I quote, and whose opportunities for forming a correct opinion are probably superior to his. The comparison I have already invited between English and foreign mathematicians will not I am persuaded tell against Euclid. Moreover the best students who come to Cambridge, by the testimony of the most eminent teachers here, come from schools and colleges in which Euclid is most strenuously maintained; it would be hardly too much to assert also the converse, that the worst students come from places where Euclid has been neglected or superseded. But let us proceed to some remarks on a direct experimental investigation. The great difficulty of conducting such a process is obvious. It will be hard to secure that pupils shall be selected of equal power, and be trained with equal assiduity; and then if one teacher is to try various methods he is liable, since he knows that a controversy is now existing as to the result, to deviate from impartiality in his treatment of the rival methods. Moreover there may naturally arise some disagreement as to the means to be used for testing the value of the results, and as to the accurate application of the principle which may be finally adopted for this end.

Something however will be gained if we settle on which side lies the duty of establishing the doctrine which it maintains.

In the first place it must be remembered that Euclid is not an unknown and an untried book. Simple as the remark is, yet many persons seem to forget how great a company of mathematicians has been trained on this system, and to what eminence not a few of them have reached. Now turn to the list of Elementary modern works on Geometry which is furnished in the first report of the Association for the Improvement of Geometrical Teaching; and take the book which stands at the head of the list, which is entitled *The Essentials of Geometry...as taught in French and German Schools.* I know nothing of this work, except that it has been severely handled in a review which is not by any means strongly biassed in favour of Euclid. However, passing by this unfortunate circumstance, still the case stands thus: we know that Euclid has been long used almost exclusively in English schools, and from these schools have issued mathematicians second to none in the world; suppose then that any sanguine friend should ascribe on theoretical grounds the highest merit to the *Essentials of Geometry*, yet the practical efficiency of this recent production must be at present, and must long remain, a matter only of hope or at most of faith.

It may be said that it is here *assumed* that Euclid has been found effectual as an introduction to Geometry; I reply that in comparing ourselves with foreigners sufficient indirect evidence has been furnished on this point.

But direct evidence is not wanting. Suppose that one of the most distinguished professors in England—whose pupils also have gained a high reputation as investigators and teachers—recommends the study of Euclid with the authority of his great attainments and experience; then this testimony cannot be set aside, until something of corresponding weight is adduced on the other side. I know that these words have been used: "We want no second Euclid set up to stay the progress of knowledge, to hamper the education of future generations, and to cumber the ground of science": but I am not aware that any evidence has been produced to bear out these charges. The history of science has perhaps not many cultivators in England; it has certainly had none in recent times superior to the professor to whom I have just alluded; his wide knowledge at least had not discovered any indications of the progress of knowledge being stayed by the adherence to Euclid. I hope I do not lay too much stress on the matured opinions of my venerated master and friend. Others also have learned to attach weight to his judgment; and a great living philosopher speaks of him as one "who combined with the attainments of a mathematician those of a philosophic logician and psychologist."

In the next place in the absence of direct experiment we may appeal to observation. During the existence of the East India Company's military college at Addiscombe, it is well known that the cadets were instructed in mathematics by the aid of a course drawn up by the late Professor Cape. The geometry in this course was of the kind which our modern reformers recommend, being founded on Legendre, and adopting the principle of hypothetical constructions which is now so emphatically praised. In certain large schools where youths were trained for the military colleges it was usual to instruct a class of candidates for Woolwich, in Euclid, and a class of candidates for Addiscombe in Cape's adaptation of Legendre. Fairness in the procedure was secured by giving the same number of hours by the same masters to each class; and the honour and rewards which attended success supplied an effectual stimulus both to teachers and pupils. Now consider the result. I was assured by a teacher who was for many years distinguished for the number and the success of his pupils, that the training acquired by the Euclid class was far superior to that acquired by the Legendre class. The Euclid was not more difficult to teach and was more potent and more beneficial in its influence. The testimony made the stronger impression on me because at the time I was disposed from theoretical considerations to hold an opposite opinion; I was inclined for example to support the use of hypothetical constructions. Such experience as I afterwards gained shewed the soundness of the judgment at which the practical teacher had arrived; and I have also received the emphatic evidence of others who had good opportunities of considering the question, and had come to the same conclusion. I have myself examined at Woolwich and at Addiscombe, and am confident that the teaching in both institutions was sound and zealous; but I have no hesitation in saying that the foundation obtained from Euclid was sounder than that from Legendre. Nor could the difference be ascribed to a difference in ability; for to say the very least the Company's service was as well supplied with candidates of general ability and of mathematical power as the Queen's.

Although several years have now passed since these observations and comparisons were made, yet there must still remain persons whose engagements enabled them to be practically conversant with the merits of the two systems of geometry; and who can therefore corroborate or challenge the conclusion which I have recorded. I would not lay undue stress on this experiment, but it was carried on for many years with all precautions for fairness; and the result must be at least as valuable as the confident prediction now hazarded as to a trial not yet made.

I must not dismiss this matter without noticing the thoroughly effective manner in which the candidates for admission to the military colleges are prepared in Euclid. A very distinguished mathematician, who has been recently engaged in examining these candidates, assured me that the performance was truly admirable; the testimony was the more striking as it was offered spontaneously, and was quite unconnected with any controversial discussion. I have been struck myself with the improvement which has occurred in the knowledge of Euclid exhibited by the men who enter the University now compared with what it was some years since.

Again, there is I think one quarter from which we may derive some useful materials for forming a judgment; I mean the academical institutions and the schools of America. I seek for information myself, for I do not possess it; but it seems to me that if the appeal were favourable to the innovators in geometry we should have heard of the result. I think that Euclid has not that prescriptive authority in America which he has with us, that there is perfect liberty as to the books and methods to be employed, so that the conditions which our reformers hold to be essential to a sound mathematical education are there secured. I have before me a work on geometry which is reported to be esteemed in America; and I see that it corresponds very fairly with the scheme which has been recommended by some of the opponents of Euclid: for instance, parallel lines are defined to be those which *have the same direction.* Now the American students and investigators being thus liberated from the obstacles which are said to " stay the progress of knowledge " with ourselves, let us consider whether their contributions to the higher departments of pure and mixed mathematics can be compared with our own. I have no wish to depreciate their labours; I know that they possess able mathematicians, and that in the department of astronomy they have produced meritorious works : but I maintain that as against us their utmost distinction almost vanishes. And yet with their great population, their abundant wealth, their attention to education, their freedom from civil and religious disabilities, and their success in literature, we might well expect the most conspicuous eminence in mathematics. However, as I have said, I leave the matter for further enquiry, especially by those who assert that we "cumber the ground of science" by adhering to Euclid.

It would be interesting and perhaps instructive to know what has led to the sudden discontent with Euclid; it is not impossible that there may be some cause which has not been prominently brought forward. Thus it has been said that one of the real objections at the present day to the classical education formerly exclusively adopted, is that it is impossible to keep out of the hands of boys the numerous accessible translations of the Latin and Greek authors, and so the study of the learned languages has now lost much of the value which formerly belonged to it as a discipline : and yet this objection has, I think, never been *publicly* advanced. Similarly, there may be some objection which has been felt, but not expressed, against the prevalence of Euclid ; it cannot be of the nature of that just indicated, because the complaint is that the usual mode of study is too difficult, not too easy : indeed tradition says, that the great master himself allowed that his was no royal road to geometry, and modern critics seem to assert also that it is not a popular road.

It is impossible to divine what may be the nature of an objection which has not been revealed; but I have sometimes been inclined to conjecture that it may be connected with the great increase of examinations in the country. In these examinations, systematic failure in certain subjects is soon detected, both by the examiners and by those who train the candidates. If the teachers learn from former experience the necessity of exerting themselves more strenuously, the desired success is soon obtained. If however the teachers are mainly interested in other subjects, and are unwilling to undergo the trouble required to ensure attention, it is natural to try to evade the difficulty by asking for a less stringent examination.

I remember once when I had been engaged in conducting a large examination where the names and schools of the candidates were altogether unknown to me, and the failures were unusually numerous, I was with much concern expressing my regret at this circumstance to the presiding authorities; the reply, however, relieved me from all anxiety, as it was to this effect : "We were fully prepared for the unfavourable result, because the list of candidates comprised a very large number from.....school." It is a matter of serious regret when the character of a very large school becomes thus unpleasantly notorious. A more agreeable example I can adduce also from my own experience in large examinations where the names and schools of the candidates were publicly recorded. It was found on more than one occasion that the pupils of a certain institution, while acquitting themselves so well in classics as to testify to the excellence of their training, failed grievously in Euclid. The attention of the teachers was drawn to this circumstance by the presiding authorities at the examination; the communication was received with grateful courtesy; and in a very short time the mathematical proficiency of the institution was worthy of its well-earned classical reputation.

Another peculiarity of the examination system is that it tests *individual* proficiency. Too often it happens in a large school that although good instruction is available for those who have the ability and inclination to attend to it, yet there is no very great pressure applied to the mass of the pupils. We hear complaints from ·the masters of large public schools that they cannot prepare youths for this and that examination; the youths go elsewhere to obtain the required training: and the process is frequently abused as *cramming*.

I have elsewhere expressed my regret at the constant employment of this absurd and unmeaning word; and need not now repeat my remarks. It will be sufficient for me to record my opinions briefly. ·I say then that the official programmes of such examinations as I have seen appear to me to be satisfactory in general, though there may be details susceptible of improvement; the manner in which the candidates acquit themselves shews that the teaching which they receive is sound and efficient, and undeserving of any opprobrious epithet; in particular the knowledge of Euclid reflects credit on the candidates and justifies the use of

11—2

this text-book; and finally that with little difficulty the system of a large public school might be so adjusted as to prepare the pupils adequately for such examinations in general.

I am disposed to think that the wide choice of studies which is now allowed and encouraged may also exercise a disastrous influence on the faith in Euclid. In former days scarcely anything but classics could be considered included in the higher English education. Then the elements of Mathematics gained a precarious footing. Now Natural Philosophy, Chemistry, and Natural History urge their claims; not to mention Modern Languages and History. I presume that all these recent subjects, so far as they can be presented to boys, are much easier than Euclid; making considerably less demand for patient continuous thought. It is not surprising then that boys shew disinclination, especially if they see that the teacher is himself a sceptic or a scoffer as to the value of the text-book he has to expound. I admit that at the outset exertion is necessary in order to penetrate into Euclid; and if a boy has full confidence in the ability and judgment of his master he is encouraged to make the necessary effort. But if there is on the part of the master a scarcely concealed wish to shew that the study is difficult and repulsive for the pupil, we cannot be surprised if the pupil himself is eager to assist in establishing such a conclusion. Even if the teacher is only languid without being positively hostile, his real sentiments are soon discovered: hypocrisy, which according to the poet cannot be detected by men or by angels, has but a slender chance of deceiving schoolboys.

I think there is reason to fear lest the privilege now so much allowed of choosing special subjects for study may tend to weaken the average powers of thought and application on the part of the young. I should not like to be misunderstood here : I admit that any of the great branches of study may become a training in its higher parts, when it is possible that original investigation can be pursued ; but I am doubtful whether this can be asserted of the rudiments. I have elsewhere maintained that it is the prerogative of the older subjects, especially of mathematics, to supply from the earliest period exercise for the reason as well as for the memory. The fact that in some schools the time of boys is now partly devoted to the classificatory sciences renders it desirable that the rigid geometry of Euclid should remain an influential element of their training. The main principles of the former pursuit are easier and more readily learned in any practical occupation ; those of the latter are more difficult, and if omitted in youth are not likely to be supplied in after life.

Perhaps the hostility to Euclid may be partly explained by the natural desire to escape from evils which are known even at the risk of encountering others still greater which are as yet unknown. When a particular method has been long used for instruction, the difficulties which belong to it become conspicuous, and amount to a formidable collection ; a mass of commentary written or traditional accumulates and is onerous both to students and teachers. The temptation is great to try some new method which promises relief from some of the familiar troubles ; even if diffi-

culties exist in the new method they are at present
dormant; time must elapse before they are aroused,
still more before, under the direction of examiners, they
become formidable: therefore for the present the advantage seems to lie on the side of novelty.   For an illustration we may observe that the Differential Calculus
was for a long time studied on the method of expansions, and the difficulties of this method pressed so
urgently on teachers that they turned gladly to the
method of limits as an improvement.   Although I have
myself published a book which has had some influence
in establishing the method of limits in England, yet I
have never thought it impossible that taste should
revert to that of expansions, at least when time had
partially effaced the memory of the objections which
had finally become so powerful.   Thus it may be
possible that many teachers under a vivid impression
of all the difficulties and objections which the experience of centuries has detected in Euclid should wish
for a new system in which faults might be removed;
forgetting how highly probable it is that a criticism as
keen and an experience as long as have been devoted
to Euclid would be effective in damaging the character
of any modern substitute.

I need only allude to the systematic elevation of
amusements into an important part of the life of a
youth, both at schools and the universities.   The
subject has been often noticed, and the fear expressed
that an appreciable fraction of the time, and a still
larger part of the spirit and energy which should be
devoted to more serious pursuits are now dissipated in
what are called athletic sports.

Although I have admitted that the study of Euclid is one that really demands patient attention from the beginner, yet I cannot admit that the tax is unreasonable. My own experience has been gained in the following manner. Some years since on being appointed principal mathematical lecturer in my college, more systematic arrangements were introduced for the lectures of the freshmen than had been previously adopted; and as the Euclid seemed to be one of the less popular subjects I undertook it myself. Thus for a long period the way in which this has been taught in schools, and the results of such teaching, have been brought under my notice. It need scarcely be said that while many of the students who have thus presented themselves to me have been distinguished for mathematical taste and power, yet the majority have been of other kinds; namely, either persons of ability whose attention was fully occupied with studies different from mathematics, or persons of scanty attainments and feeble power who could do little more than pass the ordinary examination. I can distinctly affirm that the cases of hopeless failure in Euclid were very few; and the advantages derived from the study, even by men of feeble ability, were most decided. In comparing the performance in Euclid with that in Arithmetic and Algebra there could be no doubt that the Euclid had made the deepest and most beneficial impression: in fact it might be asserted that this constituted by far the most valuable part of the whole training to which such persons were subjected. Even the modes of expression in Euclid, which have been theoretically condemned as long and wearisome, seemed to be in practice well adapted to the position of beginners. As I have already stated there appears to me a decided improvement gradually taking place in the knowledge of the subject exhibited by youths on entering the University. My deliberate judgment is that our ordinary students would suffer very considerably if instead of the well-reasoned system of Euclid any of the more popular but less rigid manuals were allowed to be taken as a substitute.

Let me now make a few remarks on the demand which has been made to allow other books instead of Euclid in *examinations.* It has been said: "We demand that we should not be,—as we are now, by the fact of Euclid being set as a text-book for so many examinations,—practically obliged to adhere to one book. Surely such a request, made by men who know what they want, and are competent to form an opinion on the subject,—and made in earnest,—should induce the Universities and other examining bodies to yield their consent." The grounds of the demand then are three; that it is made in earnest, that it is made by those who know what they want, and that it is made by those who are competent to form an opinion on the subject. I need not delay on two of the grounds; the experience of every day shews that claimants may know what they want, and be terribly in earnest in their solicitations, and yet it may be the duty of those to whom the appeal is made to resist it. Moreover it is obvious that the adoption of Euclid as a text-book is prescribed by those who are equally in earnest and know what they recommend. In short if no institution is to be defended when it is attacked knowingly and earnestly, it is plain that no institution is safe.

I turn then to the other ground, namely that the demand is made by men who are competent to form an opinion on the subject. Now it is not for me to affect to speak in the name of the University of Cambridge; mine is the opinion of only a private unofficial resident. But I have little doubt that many persons here will maintain, without questioning the competence of the claimants to form an opinion, that we ourselves are still much more competent to form an opinion.

For it will not be denied that in all which relates to mathematical knowledge we have an aggregate of eminence which far surpasses what has yet been collected together to press the demand on the University. Moreover as inspectors and judges we occupy a central position as it were, and thus enjoy opportunities which do not fall to isolated teachers however eminent and experienced. The incessant demands made upon the University to furnish examiners for schools and for the local examinations keep us as a body practically familiar with the standard of excellence attained in various places of instruction. Then as college lecturers and private tutors we have the strongest motives for keenly discriminating the state of mathematical knowledge in different schools, as shewn by the performance of the candidates when brought under our notice. Moreover some of the residents in the University by continued intercourse with old pupils, now themselves occupying important positions as teachers, are enabled to prolong and enlarge the experience which they may have already obtained directly or indirectly. If it is obvious that certain teachers by ability and devotion have for many years sent up well-trained pupils, the University may well consider that it would be neither right nor wise to deprive its best friends of their justly earned distinction, by relaxing in any way the rigour of the examinations. Instead then of urging an instant acquiescence with demands on the ground that those who make them are well qualified to judge, the claimants should endeavour by *argument* to convince others who are still better qualified to judge.

Here let me invite attention to the following remark which has been made in support of the claim: " In every other subject this is freely accorded ; we are not obliged to use certain grammars or dictionaries, or one fixed treatise on arithmetic, algebra, trigonometry, chemistry, or any other branch of science. Why are we to be tied to one book in geometry alone ?" Now in the first place it may be said that there are great advantages in the general use of one common book; and that when one book has long been used almost exclusively it would be rash to throw away certain good in order to grasp at phantasmal benefits. So well is this principle established that we have seen in recent times a vigorous, and it would seem successful effort, to secure the use of a common Latin Grammar in the eminent public schools. In the second place the analogy which is adduced in the remark quoted above would be rejected by many persons as involving an obvious fallacy, namely that the word *geometry* denotes the same thing by all who use it. By the admirers of Euclid it means a system of demonstrated propositions valued more for the process of reasoning involved than for the results obtained. Whereas with some of the modern reformers the rigour of the method is of small account compared with the facts themselves. We have only to consult the modern books named in a certain list, beginning with the *Essentials of Geometry*, to see that practically the object of some of our reformers is not to teach the same subject with the aid of a different text-book, but to teach something very different from what is found in Euclid, under the common name of geometry.

It may be said that I am *assuming* the point in question, namely that Euclid is the best book in geometry; but this is not the case. I am not an advocate for *finality* in this matter; though I do go so far as to say that a book should be *decidedly* better than Euclid before we give up the advantages of uniformity which it will be almost impossible to secure if the present system is abandoned. But, as it has been well observed by one of the most distinguished mathematicians in Cambridge, "The demand is unreasonable to throw aside Euclid in favour of any compendium however meagre and however unsound; and this is really the demand which is made : it will be time enough to consider about the discontinuance of Euclid when a better book is deliberately offered." It may be added that the superiority to Euclid must be established by indisputable evidence; not by the author's own estimation, the natural but partial testimony of parental fondness; not by the hasty prediction of some anonymous and irresponsible reviewer ; not by the authority of eminent men unless the eminence is founded on mathematical attainments ; not even by the verdict of teachers who are not conspicuous for the success of their pupils. The decision must rest with students, teachers, and examiners, of considerable reputation in the range of the mathematical sciences.

It must be allowed that there is diversity of opinion among the opponents of Euclid, for while the majority seem to claim freedom in the use of any text-books they please, others rather advocate the construction and general adoption of a new text-book. The former class on the whole seem to want something easier and more popular than Euclid; among the latter class there are a few whose notion seems to be that the text-book should be more rigorous and more extensive than Euclid. There are various considerations which seem to me to indicate that if a change be made it will not be in the direction of *greater rigour;* the origin of the movement, the character of the text-books which have hitherto been issued, and the pressure of more modern and more attractive studies, combine to warn us that if the traditional authority which belongs to Euclid be abandoned, geometry will be compelled to occupy a position in general education much inferior to that which it now holds. One able and enthusiastic teacher with whom I have been in correspondence wishes to have Logic taught in conjunction with Geometry, and advocates the construction of a new text-book on this principle: it seems to me however that besieged as schoolmasters now are by the pertinacious claims of many attractive studies, it must be long before logic can force an admission into the course of instruction.

There is one very obvious mode of advancing the cause of the anti-Euclidean party, which I believe will do far more for them than the most confident assertions and predictions of the merits of the course which they advocate : let them train youths on their system to gain the highest places in the Cambridge Mathematical Tripos, and then other teachers will readily follow in the path thus opened to distinction. But it may naturally be said that as long as Euclid is prescribed for the text-book, the conditions of competition are unfair towards those who adopt some modern substitute; I will examine this point. In the Cambridge Examination for Mathematical Honours there are at present sixteen papers; a quarter of the first paper is devoted to book-work questions on Euclid. Now suppose that 1000 marks are assigned to the whole examination, and that about five of these fall to the book-work in Euclid. A student of any modern system would surely be able to secure some of these five marks, even from a stern Euclidean partisan. But to take the worst case, suppose the candidate deliberately rejects all chance of these five marks, and turns to the other matter on the paper, especially to the problems; here the advantage will be irresistibly on his side owing to the "superiority of the modern to the ancient methods of geometry" which is confidently asserted. It must be remembered that in spite of all warning and commands to the contrary, examiners will persist in making their papers longer than can be treated fully in the assigned time, so that the sacrifice of the book-work will be in itself trifling and will be abundantly compensated by the greater facility at the solution of problems which is claimed for the modern teaching, as compared with the "unsuggestiveness" of Euclid, and by the greater accuracy of reasoning, since we are told that "the logical training to be got from Euclid is very imperfect and in some respects bad." Thus on the whole the disciple of the modern school will even in the first paper of the Cambridge Tripos Examination be more favourably situated than the student of Euclid; and of course in the other papers the advantages in his favour become largely increased. For we must remember that we are expressly told that Euclid is "an unsuitable preparation for the higher mathematical training of the present day;" and that "those who continue their mathematical reading with a view of obtaining honours at the University... will gain much through economy of time and the advantage of modern lights."

The final result is this; according to the promises of the geometrical reformers, one of their pupils might sacrifice five marks out of a thousand, while for all the remaining 995 his chance would be superior to that of a Euclid-trained student. It may be added that in future the Cambridge Mathematical Examinations are to be rather longer than they have been up to the date of my writing; so that the advantage of the anti-Euclidean school will be increased. Moreover we must remember that in the Smith's Prizes Examination the elementary geometry of Euclid scarcely appears, so that the modern reformers would not have here any obstacle to the triumphant vindication of their superiority as teachers of the higher mathematics. The marvellous thing is that in these days of competition for educational prizes those who believe themselves to possess such a vast superiority of methods do not keep the secret to themselves, instead of offering it to all, and pressing it on the reluctant and incredulous. Surely instead of mere *assertion* of the benefits to be secured by the modern treatment, it will be far more dignified and far more conclusive to *demonstrate* the proposition by brilliant success in the Cambridge Mathematical Tripos. Suppose we were to read in the ordinary channels of information some such notice as this next January: " The first six wranglers are considered to owe much of their success to the fact that in their training the fossil geometry of Alexandria was thrown aside and recent specimens substituted;" then opposition would be vanquished, and teachers would wonder, praise, and imitate. But until the promises of success are followed by a performance as yet never witnessed we are reminded of the case of a bald hairdresser who presses on his customers his infallible specific for producing redundant locks. To put the question in a practical shape : let there be a large school, where Euclid is taught in purity and power ; and suppose that this school sends to the University senior wrangler after senior wrangler, together with many others of scarcely inferior position, and moreover that this success is gained without any sacrifice of classics and natural science. Again let there be another school of about the same extent as the former, which, as to all external circumstances, appears to have an obvious advantage over the former; suppose that here the modern text-books of geometry are vehemently enforced, and that in the higher places of the Cambridge Mathematical Tripos this school is almost unrepresented. Then I say that the merits of the new system as compared with those of the old are conspicuous by their absence.

It is obvious that a body like the University of Cambridge cannot be fairly expected to yield to any influence but that of argument. No part of the system of education and examination would be safe if the first attack is to be the signal of compromise or surrender. For an example consider the subject of Geometrical Conic Sections. How easy it will be to assert that this is an undesirable peculiarity of Cambridge instruction, which is scarcely known abroad, and that we cannot expect to compete with foreign nations unless we conform our methods to theirs. Or to take a still more striking example, let us refer to our study of certain portions of Newton's Principia; some persons might say that the term *insane delusion* is just as applicable here as to our retention of Euclid. It may be that the faults in more than half the productions of English mathematicians, of which we have heard, may really be due not to the text-book used for elementary geometry but to the sections of the Principia which are retained in our mathematical course.

It may be necessary to say, for those who are not acquainted with the subject, that changes in the studies at Cambridge are made by the authority of the Senate; and that among the residents at the University will be found a body of mathematicians who as students and teachers are probably to say the least equal to those of any academical institution in the world. Far different is the authority which attaches to some other colleges or universities. It might be possible on investigation to find that the decision in some cases as to the course of instruction rests with a body containing a very small number of persons known as writers on mathematics, and not one with any experience as a teacher or examiner.

As I have already hinted, the opponents of Euclid may be divided into two classes. One class, apparently the less in number, but by far the most conspicuous for attainments, obviously condemn Euclid as an inadequate course of geometry. I will venture to quote a few words pronounced before a section of the British Association by one whose brilliant genius and wide attainments have no admirer more fervent, nor pupil more grateful than myself: "I should rejoice to see... ...Euclid honourably shelved or buried 'deeper than did ever plummet sound' out of the schoolboy's reach ; morphology introduced into the elements of Algebra ; projection, correlation, and motion accepted as aids to geometry ; the mind of the student quickened and elevated and his faith awakened by early initiation into the ruling ideas of polarity, continuity, infinity, and familiarization with the doctrine of the imaginary and inconceivable."

And again : "The early study of Euclid made me a hater of geometry...."

The grounds of this dislike to Euclid are not stated. Perhaps we have only the repugnance to elementary text-books which might naturally be felt by a creative mind conscious of the power to advance without any superfluous aid; tradition seems to record such characteristics of Newton and of Pascal. It would be unwise, however, to suppose that such exceptional cases are likely to be common. But, whatever may have produced the dislike to Euclid in the illustrious mathematician whose words I have quoted, there is no ground for supposing that he would have been better pleased with the substitutes which are now offered and recommended in its place. But the remark which is naturally suggested by the passages, is that nothing prevents an enthusiastic teacher from carrying his pupils to any height he pleases in Geometry, even if he starts with the use of Euclid. I take it as obvious that the *real* and the *conceivable* must precede the *imaginary* and the *inconceivable* in the course of instruction; and then it is difficult to see what is the objection to retaining Euclid for this humble introductory function. At least this may be said; the words of the eminent mathematician cannot be quoted against Euclid, in comparison with a rival elementary text-book, unless the modern work expounds polarity, continuity, infinity, together with the imaginary and inconceivable.

To those who object to Euclid as an inadequate course of plane geometry it may then be replied briefly that it is easy, if thought convenient or necessary, to supply any additional matter. But for my part I think there are grave objections to any large increase in the extent of the course of synthetical geometry which is to be prepared for examination purposes. One great drawback to our present system of mathematical instruction and examination is the monotony which prevails in many parts. When a mathematical subject has been studied so far as to master the essential principles, little more is gained by pursuing these principles into almost endless applications. On this account we may be disposed to regard with slender satisfaction the expenditure of much time on geometrical conic sections; the student seems to gain only new facts, but no fresh ideas or principles. Thus after a moderate course of synthetical geometry such as Euclid supplies, it may be most advantageous for the student to pass on to other subjects like analytical geometry and trigonometry which present him with ideas of another kind, and not mere repetitions of those with which he is already familiar.

However, as I have said, the objection to Euclid seems to be more commonly that it is too difficult and too elaborate, than that it is inadequate; and the answer may reasonably be given that if Euclid be abandoned it will probably be difficult to retain any exact system of geometry at all. The claims of the natural sciences are so vigorously urged that all the older subjects of study are in danger of being displaced. But if in any school or academic institution an exact and rigorous system of geometry is advisable, it would seem to be eminently so where the natural sciences are regarded with conspicuous favour. We may readily admit that any study pursued by an earnest man as an investigator will be an adequate discipline for him; and yet we may contend that there will be a wide difference between the training obtained from different subjects when they are taught to others. Much that is valuable when gained by personal research may be of no utility when received from a lecturer or teacher. The natural history sciences, as they must be presented to boys, seem to me to fall far below the ancient languages and mathematics as instruments of education. There is, I think, little in *elementary* natural history which corresponds to the effort required in mastering an important demonstration; and nothing which can call forth the faculty of original thought and combination of known truths like the problems and exercises of mathematics.

It has been said, and apparently with great justice, that examination in elementary geometry under a system of unrestricted text-books will be a very troublesome process; for it is obvious that in different systems the demonstration of a particular proposition may be more or less laborious, and so may be entitled to more or fewer marks. This perplexity is certainly felt by examiners as regards geometrical conic sections; and by teachers also who may be uncertain as to the particular system which the examiners may prefer or favour. It has been *asserted* that the objection thus raised is imaginary and that "the manuals of geometry will not differ from one another nearly so widely as the manuals of algebra or chemistry : yet it is not difficult to examine in algebra and chemistry." But I am unable to feel the confidence thus expressed. It seems to me that much more variety may be expected in treatises on geometry than on algebra; certainly if we may judge from the experience of the examiners at Cambridge the subject of geometrical conics is the most embarrassing which occurs at present, and this fact suggests a conclusion very different from that which is laid down in the preceding quotation. Of course there will be no trouble in examining a single school because the system there adopted will be known and followed by the examiner.

I have no wish to exaggerate the difficulty; but I consider it to be real and serious, more especially as it presents itself at the outset of a youth's career, and so may cause disappointment just when discriminating encouragement is most valuable. But I think the matter must be left almost entirely to the discretion of examiners; the attempts which have been made to settle it by regulation do not seem to me very happy. For example, I read : " As the existing text-books are not very numerous, it would not be too much to require examiners to be acquainted with them sufficiently for the purpose of testing the accuracy of written, or even, if necessary, of oral answers." The language seems to me truly extraordinary. Surely examiners are in general men of more mathematical attainments than this implies ; for it would appear that all we can expect them to do is to turn to some text-book and see if the student has correctly reproduced it. The process in a *viva voce* examination would be rather ignominious if when an answer had been returned by a candidate some indifferent manual had to be consulted to see if the answer was correct.

I have heard that an examining board has recently issued instructions to its executive officers to make themselves acquainted with the various text-books. This does not enjoin distinctly, what the above quotation implies, that the examiner is to accept all demonstrations which are in print as of nearly equal value ; but it seems rather to suggest such a course. The point is important and should be settled. Suppose a candidate offered something taken from the *Essentials of Geometry,* and the examiner was convinced that the treatment was inadequate or unsound ; then is the candidate nevertheless to obtain full marks ? Again, it may be asked, why printed books alone are to be accepted ;

and why a student who has gone through a manuscript course of geometry should be precluded from following it ? The regulation might be made that he should submit a copy of his manuscript course to the examiner in order that it might be ascertained whether he had reproduced it accurately. As I have already intimated, the only plan which can be adopted is to choose able and impartial men for examiners, and trust them to appreciate the merits of the papers submitted by the candidates to them.

The examiners will find many perplexing cases I have no doubt ; one great source of trouble seems to me to consist in the fact that what may be a sound demonstration to one person with adequate preliminary study is not a demonstration to another person who has not gone through the discipline. To take a very simple example, let the proposition be ; *the angles at the base of an isosceles triangle are equal.* Suppose a candidate dismisses this briefly with the words, *this is evident from symmetry;* the question will be, what amount of credit is to be assigned to him. It is quite possible that a well-trained mathematician may hold himself convinced of the truth of the proposition by the consideration of symmetry, but it does not follow that the statement would really be a demonstration for an early student. Or suppose that another imbued with " the doctrine of the imaginary and inconceivable " says as briefly " the proposition is true, for the inequality of the angles is inconceivable and therefore false; " then is the examiner to award full marks, even if he himself belongs to the school of metaphysics which denies that the inconceivable is necessarily the false ?

I do not wish to dwell here on the principle that the conviction produced by a demonstration depends much or mainly on the state of the mind of the person to whom it is offered; but one remark in illustration may be made. Our text-books sometimes give us investigations in which processes really belonging to the Differential Calculus are forced into an elementary geometrical form, professedly for the benefit of those who are not yet acquainted with the Differential Calculus. However satisfactory the demonstrations may be to those who construct them, I am disposed to think them very ineffective to the persons for whom they are designed. But to keep within our present subject, let us turn to Euclid i. 13 ; this is held to be superfluous by some critics because the fact is self-evident. To a student who has a good notion of *an angle of* 180 *degrees,* in the language of Trigonometry, it may be evident that he has the same aggregate whether he cuts his angle into two equal angles or into two unequal angles. But the notion of *an angle of* 180 *degrees* is not perhaps very obvious to a beginner; he is apt to consider it a contradiction to speak of an angle when he sees no opening : accordingly Euclid may reasonably avoid at this stage the introduction of the notion.

It is obvious that when we have one text-book in common use, as in the case of Euclid, the experience of teachers and examiners enables them to judge of the degree of conviction which the demonstrations bring with them much better than when their attention is distracted by numerous rivals each offering a special system.

It may be expedient to notice briefly some of the objections in detail which have been urged against Euclid.

I begin with one which I cannot discuss, because I do not understand it, and this is unfortunate because it is said to be "the worst of all;" however the reader may try for himself:—"it wants life and freshness. These last are qualities which cannot be imparted to it, even by the best of teachers, so long as the exact order and words of the book are demanded in examinations." I cannot interpret the metaphorical language "life and freshness", which may probably be applicable to any thing which boys are set to learn, as for instance the Latin Grammar. The meaning which seems suggested by the following words is that "life and freshness" are wanting where examiners are too strict; but then whatever text-book is adopted examiners must maintain some standard of accuracy, which must be fixed by their own judgment, or by tradition, or by official regulations. Moreover I presume that in general each student will confine himself to some *one* text-book, and then it is not obvious how he is more fortunate with respect to "life and freshness" than if he used Euclid ; for it can scarcely be supposed a judicious employment of his time to conduct him through various elementary treatises on the same subject. Perhaps after all this worst defect in Euclid merely means that Examiners are now too strict, and will become more lax when this book is no longer essential ; then many persons will be inclined to look on the change as the worst evil which the so-called reform would introduce.

It has been urged as an objection against Euclid

that the number of his propositions is too great. Thus
it has been said that the 173 propositions of the six
books might be reduced to 120, and taught in very
little more than half the time required to go through
the same matter in Euclid. So far as the *half time* is
concerned this seems to be only an expression of belief
as to the result of an untried experiment ; it is based
on the comparison of a few other books with Euclid,
one of these being the Course of the late Professor
Cape ; as I have already stated, actual experience suggests a conclusion directly contrary to the present prediction. As to the *number* of propositions we may
readily admit that a reduction might be made, for it is
obvious that we may in many cases either combine or
separate according to our taste. But the difficulty of
a subject does not vary directly as the number of propositions in which it is contained ; a single proposition
will in some cases require more time and attention
than half-a-dozen others. I have no doubt that the
mixture of easy propositions with the more difficult is
a great encouragement to beginners in Euclid ; and
instead of diminishing the number of propositions I
should prefer to see some increase : for example I
should like to have Euclid I. 26 divided into two parts
and Euclid I. 28 into two parts.

Again it has been said that Euclid is artificial, and
that he has "sacrificed to a great extent simplicity and
naturalness in his demonstrations ;" it is a curious instance of the difference of opinion which we may find
on the same subject, for, with a much wider experience
than the writer whom I quote, I believe that Euclid
maintains, and does not sacrifice, simplicity and natu-

ralness in his system, assuming that we wish to have strictness above all things.

The exclusion of hypothetical constructions has been represented as a great defect in Euclid; and it has been said that this has made the *confused order* of his first book necessary. Confused order is rather a contradictory expression; but it may be presumed that the charge is intended to be one of confusion: I venture to deny the confusion. I admit that Euclid wished to make the subject depend on as few axioms and postulates as possible; and this I regard as one of his great merits; it has been shewn by one of the most distinguished mathematicians of our time how the history of science teaches in the clearest language that the struggle against self-imposed restrictions has been of the most signal service in the advancement of knowledge.

The use of hypothetical constructions will not present itself often enough to produce any very great saving in the demonstrations; while the difficulty which they produce to many beginners, as shewn by the experience to which I have already referred, is a fatal objection to them. Why should a beginner not assume that he can draw a circle through four given points if he finds it convenient? This illustration was given to me by an examiner of eminent ability and long standing after I had myself selected it. We may be told that French teachers find no trouble in the use of the hypothetical constructions; but then we do not know enough of the circumstances to make the comparison fairly. The boys in France may give more time to the subject than is usually devoted to it in our large public schools; and they may derive from other studies a logical training which is not common among ourselves: it is a fact for example that they give a close attention to their own language which has not a parallel in our cultivation of English. Finally I hold that Euclid, in his solution of the problems he requires, supplies matter which is simple and attractive to beginners, and which therefore adds practically nothing to their labours, while it has the advantage of rendering his treatise far more rigorous and convincing to them.

The objections against Euclid's order seem to me to spring mainly from an intrusion of natural history into the region of mathematics; I am not the first to print this remark though it occurred to me independently. It is to the influence of the classificatory sciences that we probably owe this notion that it is desirable or essential in our geometrical course to have all the properties of triangles thrown together, then all the properties of rectangles, then perhaps all the properties of circles; and so on. Let me quote authority in favour of Euclid, far more impressive than any which on this point has been brought against him: "Euclid...fortunately for us, never dreamed of a geometry of triangles as distinguished from a geometry of circles,...but made one help out the other as he best could."

Euclid has been blamed for his adherence to the syllogistic method; but it is not necessary to say much on this point, because the reformers are not agreed concerning it: those who are against the syllogism may pair off with those who are for the syllogism. We are told in this connexion that, "the result is, as every one knows, that boys may have worked at Euclid for years, and may yet know next to nothing of Geometry." We may readily admit that such may be the case with boys exceptionally stupid or indolent; but if any teacher records this as the average result of his experience, it must I think be singularly to his own discredit.

There is, I see, a notion that the syllogistic form, since it makes the demonstrations a little longer, makes them more difficult; this I cannot admit. The number of words employed is not a test of the difficulty of a demonstration. An examiner, especially if he is examining *viva voce*, can readily find out where the difficulties of the demonstrations really lie; my own experience leads me to the conclusion that the syllogistic form instead of being an impediment is really a great assistance, especially to early students.

"Unsuggestiveness" has been urged as a fault in Euclid; which is interpreted to mean that it does not produce ability to solve problems. We are told: "Everybody recollects, even if he have not the daily experience, how unavailable for problems a boy's knowledge of Euclid generally is. Yet this is the true test of geometrical knowledge; and problems and original work ought to occupy a much larger share of a boy's time than they do at present." I need not repeat what I have already said, that English mathematicians, hitherto trained in Euclid, are unrivalled for their ingenuity and fertility in the construction and solution of problems. But I will remark that in the important mathematical examinations which are conducted at Cambridge the rapid and correct solution of problems is of paramount value, so that any teacher who can develop that power in his pupils will need no other evidence of the merits of his system.

Euclid's treatment of proportion has been especially marked out for condemnation; indeed with the boldness which attaches to many assertions on the subject of elementary geometry, it has been pronounced already *dead.* In my own college it has never been laid aside; only a few months since one of our most influential tutors stated that he was accustomed to give a proposition out of the fifth book of Euclid, to some candidates for emoluments, and he considered it a very satisfactory constituent of the whole process of testing them.

I should exceedingly regret the omission of the fifth book of Euclid, which I hold to be one of the most important parts of the training supplied by Elementary Geometry. I do not consider it necessary for beginners to go through the entire book; but the leading propositions might be mastered, and the student led to see how they can be developed if necessary. I may refer here to some valuable remarks which have been made on the subject by the writer of a *Syllabus of Elementary Geometry*...who himself I believe counts with the reformers. He sums up thus :..."any easy and unsatisfactory short cuts (and I have sometimes seen an inclination for such), should be scouted, as a simple deception of inexperienced students."

However, I must remark that I see with great satisfaction the following *Resolution* which was adopted at a recent meeting of the *Association for the Improvement of Geometrical Teaching:* "That no treatise on geometry can be regarded as complete without a rigorous treatment of ratio and proportion either by Euclid's method, or by some equally rigorous method of limits." It would be injudicious to lay much stress on resolutions carried by a majority of votes; but at least we have a striking contradiction to the confident statement that Euclid's theory of proportion is *dead*. We shall very likely see here, what has been noticed before, that a course may be proposed which differs widely from Euclid's, and then under the guidance of superior knowledge and experience, the wanderers are brought back to the old path. Legendre's return to Euclid's treatment of parallels is a conspicuous example; see the valuable paper by Professor Kelland on *Superposition* in the *Edinburgh Transactions*, Vol. XXI.

I cannot avoid noticing one objection which has been urged against Euclid in relation to his doctrine of proportion; namely, that it leaves "the half-defined impression that all profound reasoning is something far-fetched and artificial, and differing altogether from good clear common sense." It appears to me that if a person imagines that "good clear common sense" will be sufficient for mastering pure and mixed mathematics, to say nothing of contributing to their progress,—the sooner he is undeceived the better. Mathematical science consists of a rich collection of investigations accumulated by the incessant labour of many years, by which results are obtained far beyond the range of unassisted common sense; of these processes Euclid's theory of proportion is a good type, and it may well be said that from the degree of reverent attention which the student devotes to it, we may in most cases form a safe estimate of his future progress in these important subjects.

Some months since, a scientific periodical contained a discussion in connexion with elementary geometry which suggests a remark of practical importance. A person asked what was the best book for him to use in teaching his son geometry, justifying the necessity of the enquiry by the statement that Euclid might now be considered quite out of consideration, since an eminent Professor whom he named had joined a teacher in a well-known school in condemning it. As the Professor was not a professor of mathematics, and the school not specially distinguished in mathematics, there might be some latent meaning different from that which appeared to be conveyed as to the overthrow of Euclid. However, the enquiry gave rise to two or three communications, including a very able one from the first writer. But what appeared singular to persons accustomed to enquiries about education was the readiness of persons to offer advice with most imperfect knowledge of the circumstances. In fact the problem proposed for solution was quite indeterminate. It was not stated whether the youth was to be educated on the principle of obtaining the best possible training, without regard to external circumstances; or whether he was to be educated with the design of working for his subsistence in some profession. It was not stated whether mathematics was to be the main instrument in the training, or only secondary and subordinate. Nor was it stated whether the boy was to be prepared for examination; and if so, whether at Cambridge or elsewhere. Practically in the absence of any controlling influence which would prescribe another course it will surely be the wisest plan to continue to use the text-book which has for centuries been connected with mathematical instruction, and which is retained in the University which for this part of knowledge is without a rival in England.

In conclusion I will say that no person can be a warmer advocate than I am for the *improvement of Geometrical Teaching;* but I think that this may be attained without the hazardous experiment of rejecting methods, the efficacy of which a long experience has abundantly demonstrated.

THE MATHEMATICAL TRIPOS.

OF the examinations with which Englishmen are at all acquainted there is probably not one that can surpass even if it can equal the mathematical tripos at Cambridge for historical interest and competitive severity. Perhaps in other countries there may be contests still more arduous and more important, as in China, or at the *Ecole Polytechnique* of Paris; but practically for us there is nothing which can stand before the Cambridge institution. No justification will therefore be necessary for a writer who proposes to offer some practical remarks on the nature of the mathematical tripos.

I shall not enter into the archæology of the subject; let it be sufficient to say that the Cambridge Calendars have preserved the lists of the successful candidates for about 120 years, arranged in the three well-known classes of wranglers, senior optimes, and junior optimes.

It would seem that the mathematical studies and honours of Cambridge rest on a foundation altogether different from that on which they were originally placed, and on which they remained during the first quarter of the present century. The mathematical sciences seem to have been cultivated formerly mainly as a discipline; not commenced in general before residence at Cambridge, and unless in a few special cases

13

not continued beyond the period of undergraduate studies. There were in fact scarcely any educational treatises on mathematics; the subjects were taught at the University mainly by lectures, and the manuscripts which the lecturers used were, at least in some cases, transmitted from one teacher to his successor in office. I remember, when an undergraduate myself, that a student came up to the University supplied with a large collection of the written notes which had guided his father's course to distinction in the previous generation; though it soon appeared that they had lost the value which they might once have possessed.

In former times a student may not unfrequently have entered the University quite ignorant of mathematics, his training having been obtained in other branches of learning, and yet have ultimately obtained the highest place in the examination. Thus Atwood who came from Westminster school was third wrangler in 1769, and Pollock who came from St Paul's school was senior wrangler in 1806; it can scarcely be doubted that both of these before they entered the University must have been almost exclusively engaged in the classical studies which were characteristic of their famous schools.

It follows naturally that as mathematical studies were regarded mainly as a discipline they were frequently entirely dropped, or indefinitely postponed, when the period of undergraduate discipline was completed. Thus high wranglers went on their way to the occupations of life; they became clergymen, schoolmasters, or lawyers: and though they may have distinguished themselves in their professions, they did not

in general exhibit any devotion to the sciences which
they had cultivated at the University. Some years
since an eminent judge who had been a high wrangler
was addressed on his retirement from the bench, in the
usual complimentary terms by the leader of the bar,
who expressed his belief that the veteran lawyer would
now return to those academical studies in which he
had gained his earliest distinction. But a frigid newspaper critic remarked that the old gentleman would
probably prefer a quiet rubber at whist to a renewal of
his acquaintance with the Differential Calculus.

In a virulent attack on the University made about
forty years since it was urged as an objection against
the system of studies that the senior wranglers did not
achieve any scientific reputation in after life. The
writer gave a list of forty senior wranglers, terminating
at the current date; and he maintained that only two
of the number had gained decisive scientific reputation;
but at least he should have remembered that the
younger men required a fair amount of time in order to
distinguish themselves : three others in his list have
since attained to eminence as mathematicians. With
audacious dexterity the pamphleteer disparaged the
University instruction by the assertion that "the most
eminent mathematician of England is at this present
time a lady": it is obvious that politeness would forbid
any examination of the truth of the assertion. I should
not have referred to an attack which is now almost
forgotten, though it excited much attention in its day,
were it not for the principle which is involved in the
writer's censure; namely that the object of the University system was mainly the production of eminent

13—2

mathematicians. It is possible that at the current date this might be apparently the tendency of the system, but I maintain it could not have been such at the date to which the assailant carried back his list. However I think there can be little doubt that at present we do practically regard mathematics not as a discipline, but rather as a business or profession. We, as it were, advertise for persons who naturally possess or have acquired by assiduous culture, mathematical power—or at least the accomplishment of passing with success through certain severe mathematical examinations. Youths who manifest any indication of the special aptitude which we value and reward are carefully trained by teachers, themselves ambitious of the reflex distinction which follows from the success of their pupils; then after due preparation they appear at the University as candidates for minor scholarships and open exhibitions, and by the combined energy of college lecturers and private tutors are stimulated and prepared during more than three years for the final struggle in the Senate House. Thus our aim seems to be not so much to afford an adequate discipline to all our students, as to lavish superfluous care upon a few, with the view of creating professional mathematicians. I am not likely to undervalue the special ability which is thus cherished, but I cannot feel that I esteem it so highly as the practice of the University really suggests. It seems to me, at least partially, to resemble the chess-playing power which we find marvellously developed in some persons; the feats which we see or know to be performed by adepts at this game are very striking, but the utility of them may be doubted, whether we regard the chess-player as an end to himself or to his country.

The change which has taken place in the nature of our mathematical studies may be seen by looking at the occupations of our high wranglers. They do not, as formerly, use their academical success as a foundation for a career in the learned professions. Out of the last twenty-five senior wranglers perhaps only two have engaged with earnestness in the study of law, and only two have taken holy orders.

Whatever then may be the theory by which we defend the prolonged cultivation of mathematics by our students, practically it seems to be the desire to produce a continuous supply of eminent masters of the subject. Without attempting to balance the loss and the gain which this practice may cause, I wish to point out that it appears to exert a damaging influence on our examination papers. There are two classes of students of very different characters who are to be tried by the same tests. There are six or eight men in every year who are competing for the highest places and for the fellowships to which such honours lead; and these for the most part have such an amount of mathematical power that very difficult papers may be submitted to them, without any extravagant disproportion, at least in quality, between what they are required to do and what they really accomplish. Then we have on the other hand a large number of students who have no particular taste for mathematics, whose attainments are gained only by patient and laborious application; for this class the papers set are on the whole far too difficult. It would seem that the examination by which we endeavour to discover who are the best possible candidates for high mathematical appointments, and the examination by which we ascertain if students of moderate ability have gone through a salutary course of discipline with steady attention, are altogether different in their objects, and can scarcely take with advantage a common form. Perhaps the consciousness that at least a few of the candidates are mathematicians of decided promise is always present to the examiners while they are constructing their papers, and on this account the problems are worked up to a high pitch of ingenious difficulty. Indeed the examination has been described by a good tempered critic as a struggle between young men who are about to take their degrees, and men a little older who have already taken their degrees ; the examiners striving to invent puzzles which shall not be easily resolved, and the candidates training themselves by long practice to solve every likely or possible form of mathematical riddle. It has been suggested that it might be expedient to have always two sets of papers produced ; one intended merely for shew to testify to the skill and resources of the examiners, and the other of a less ambitious character designed solely to be worked by the candidates.

There is no restriction as to age in our examinations for Mathematical Honours ; and in fact we sometimes find that a high place is gained by a student who may be somewhat older than the average of his competitors. The case however is comparatively rare. In the first place, the scholarships and exhibitions which are now so extensively employed to tempt persons to become members of particular colleges are almost always limited

to those who are under some specified age ; so that
there is a strong inducement to enter early on the
University course. Then there is the natural desire
to start as soon as possible on the professional occupations of life. Moreover, experience shews that for
examination purposes the vigour and elasticity of youth
are in general more serviceable than the maturer power
of older years with the almost necessary drawback of
the decline in freshness and spirit. As a matter of
experience we know that a candidate who has entered
the University rather later in life than his rivals
scarcely ever reaches the highest place. Some years
since, a father and a son came to the University in
the same year ; and report said the senior student
declined to compete for University honours on the
ground that it would be unfair to the younger men ;
but the younger men themselves rather derided than
approved the self-denial of the ancient worthy. However, without relying on report we may point to a case
in which a mathematician probably unsurpassed in the
present century but considerably older than the other
candidates attained only the fourth place.

It is perhaps not difficult to account in most instances where it occurs, for the delay of two or three
years beyond the usual age in entering the University.
A private student finds by some accident that mathematics have an attraction for him; as soon as he has
made some progress in the subject, it becomes obvious
to him that Cambridge has almost a monopoly of
mathematical distinction in England, so that it will
be nearly in vain for him to seek for any employment
in which mathematical knowledge is essential unless he

is a Cambridge graduate. Some years since an eminent
member of the non-academical school of mathematicians
was bitterly vexed at finding a person who had taken
very moderate honours at Cambridge preferred to
himself for some subordinate educational appointment
in one of the Government institutions. There was
some sort of examination test applied, and the trained
university man not unnaturally seemed to acquit himself better than the self-taught genius. A few years
later the disappointed applicant succeeded in obtaining
a similar post; but a premature death cut short a
career of great promise. In such a case the failure at
the first trial does not imply any blame on the authorities who decided the matter; they acted on fixed
principles, which are well justified by the general results to which they lead. But the example well illus-
trates the remark which has been made, namely, that
a student of mathematics has practically no choice; he
must enter the University and compete with those who
though somewhat younger than himself, may have
really devoted more time to their studies, and have
enjoyed far greater advantages in guidance and assistance.

There is however in relation to this subject a remark which must be made in order to correct the
extreme ignorance or unfairness which is sometimes
exhibited. We may find that a youth has spent some
time at one of the Scotch Universities, or at some
modern institution such as University College, London,
or Owens College, Manchester; he afterwards enters
Cambridge, at about the usual age, and gains the
highest distinction. Then we may see some remarks

in the newspapers, suggesting and complaining that such a candidate has enjoyed superior advantages to his competitors. Nothing can be more absurd ; for those who start at about the same age are as far as possible on equal terms. Parents naturally endeavour to secure for their sons the best training which is accessible ; it may be presumed that the value will be measured by the cost, and then the advantage will be on the side of the great public schools. Those who from considerations of economy or of local convenience are placed at one of the Universities or colleges to which reference has been made cannot be said to enjoy any superiority in this respect. The great public schools by reason of their ancient fame, the ample emoluments which they can offer to teachers, and the numerous pupils they can command, ought to maintain their ground with ease against any of the institutions which train pupils of about the same age. The personal assistance and superintendence which the public schools can afford to bestow, ought to be much more effective than the mere attendance at lectures, which is all that the economy of the rival institutions will in general involve.

However, leaving these subordinate matters, let us now proceed with our main subject. It is probable that many changes may have been made in the examination during the century and a quarter for which the wranglers, senior optimes, and junior optimes are recorded in the Cambridge Calendar; but I shall confine myself here and throughout the essay to matters which have fallen under my own observation and reflection.

Let me first speak of the mode of examination which ended in 1847 after being carried on for nearly ten years. The examination then continued during six days ; there were twelve papers, some to be answered in three hours, and some in two hours and a half. Three of these papers were devoted to problems, that is to original exercises specially framed for the purpose. The other nine papers were what are called *book-work* papers ; that is they consisted of questions which a candidate is supposed to be able to answer from his knowledge of the text-books. Occasionally to a book-work question a simple illustrative example is added, which is technically called a *rider*, and theoretically follows obviously from the book-work question. Let us then take the papers set in one year, for example the year 1843, which falls at about the middle of the period we are now considering. The following characteristics will at once strike a person accustomed to the style of examination which is current at the present time : the book-work questions are almost always taken directly from the text-books, and the riders are few in number and of evident simplicity. For instance, the first paper contains sixteen questions ; not more than half of them have any supplementary exercise attached to them, and all of these are of a very easy nature. The range of subjects includes physical astronomy and the undulatory theory, both of which are treated with close adherence to the recognised academical treatises of the period.

A change in the mode of examination took place after 1847 : it was then determined that the duration should be extended to eight days. First three days were to be devoted to the elementary subjects ; then an interval of rather more than a week was interposed, after which those who had passed in a satisfactory manner through the three days' test were examined during five days in the higher subjects. The new regulations were issued after the examination in 1847, and were to be brought into operation for the first time in 1848 ; so sudden a change in an important University examination has not been made on any other occasion within my experience. I cannot say positively what was the cause of the unusual haste in effecting the change, for I was an undergraduate at the date, and therefore not acquainted with the opinions of the academic rulers. A report was current, which I record with some hesitation, that the recent examiners were much dissatisfied with the performance of the candidates in the elementary subjects ; these appeared to be neglected or forgotten by ambitious students who pushed forward to the higher subjects which naturally were expected to produce more marks. Hence it was resolved to secure in future due attention to the early part of the course by compelling candidates to pass in this to the satisfaction of the examiners before they could proceed to the later part.

As a specimen of the papers which were set during the period we are now considering we may take those of 1859, which is about the middle year. Then it is obvious at a glance that almost every question which is theoretically of a book-work character is followed by a rider ; thus in the first paper of the three days there are 12 questions, and 11 of them have riders ; in the first paper of the five days there are 11 questions and

10 of them have riders. A closer inspection will shew that the questions which profess to be book-work are no longer simple extracts from the current academical treatises, but are elaborately constructed so as to assume as far as possible a new aspect; and thus to the wondering eyes of an earlier generation they might appear to be problems. The so-called riders are now in some respects more difficult than problems; for while a student is unfettered as to the mode in which he chooses to treat a problem, he is theoretically required to make the rider depend in some way on the book-work question to which it is attached. In earlier days the connection between the two was generally obvious enough to assist the candidate; but now it is not unfrequently very difficult to trace the influence of the book-work on the rider. Perhaps the supply of natural and easy inferences has been exhausted, and thus examiners have been driven to the harder exercises which they now furnish. A distinguished living mathematician is reported to have been the first who reversed the natural process in the formation of the binary compound; instead of selecting a book-work question and then constructing a simple rider to it, he is said to have invented the rider first and then sought for the piece of book-work to which it might be least unnaturally attached.

The mode of examination which commenced in 1848 endured until 1872; a quarter of a century may be considered a respectable age for any institution in these revolutionary times. During this period a gradual change has taken place in the papers; theoretically the range of subjects may have remained the same but almost every subject has expanded considerably. To take a single example ; Analytical Conic Sections so far as its principles are concerned, might have been formerly comprised within a hundred octavo pages, but now it would occupy four times that space ; while considered as a vehicle for problems it has increased in a still greater proportion. The intensity of the competition seems to have augmented ; and this for various reasons. The value of a fellowship has become in many cases nearly double of what it was ; while the number of fellowships remains the same. The minor scholarships and exhibitions have led masters to train pupils from an early period with a view to Cambridge examinations. From all parts of the world able and ambitious candidates crowd to these modern Olympian contests. While I write the latest list of mathematical honours has been published ; among the most distinguished places I see representatives of England, Wales, Ireland, America and Australia. Thus although the *number* of wranglers may not have undergone much change, yet as these wranglers are now selected from a wider area, the competitive struggle naturally becomes fiercer ; and this tends to increase the difficulty of the examination papers, because easy questions would practically leave the high men unseparated.

During the quarter of a century which has just terminated the character of the examination papers has for the most part varied gradually, without yielding much to the influence of positive enactment. Some little control has however been exercised by the interposition of the University, and this deserves to be considered.

A Board of mathematical studies has been established in the University, and theoretically large functions have been entrusted to the Board. One of the most important is the regulation of the mathematical lectures, with the view of ensuring a due representation of all the subjects: it does not however appear that the Board has ever paid the least attention to this part of its commission. The Board was accustomed to issue an annual report; this was carried on from 1849 until 1860, and then the obligation of an annual publication was relaxed; a suspicion seems to have grown up in the University that the desire to say something led to injurious activity, and that Boards like rattlesnakes are mischievous when they are not torpid. The Mathematical Board agitated two questions without bringing them to an effective result. One of these was the interposition of a few months, instead of a few days, between the two parts of the examination devoted respectively to the lower and the higher subjects. The other was the introduction of a *viva voce* element into the examination. The latter may be considered the main article of faith with the Board during the period of these annual expositions: it is first mentioned in the report of 1853; and there it is said that the members "were nearly unanimous in the opinion that such an addition to the Examination now existing would be an improvement"; and the matter appears also in the reports of 1854, 1858, 1859 and 1860.

Of late years the proposal to introduce a *viva voce* element has not been much urged: I have discussed the question elsewhere, and will here only record my opinion that whatever may be the theoretical advantages yet the practical difficulties are very great, and probably insuperable.

Let us however advert to some of the definite recommendations of the Board which were carried into practice.

In the Report of 1849 we read the following :

" Taking into consideration the great number of subjects which now occupy the attention of the candidates, and the doubt which exists as to the range of subjects from which questions may be proposed, the Board recommend that the Mathematical Theories of Electricity, Magnetism, and Heat, be not admitted as subjects of examination." And the report of 1850 recommended the following subjects to be omitted : Elliptic Functions, Laplace's Coefficients, Capillary Attraction, and the Figure of the Earth considered as heterogeneous. The Reports of 1849 and 1850 bear the signatures of some very eminent mathematicians including those of Professors Challis, Stokes, and Adams.

The subjects named in these reports as desirable to be omitted accordingly disappeared from the examination papers; but those which remained appear to have formed a course quite adequate to the wants of the examiners and the energies of the students.

Some other points brought to view in these Reports may be briefly noticed here.

Many years since it was the practice to arrange candidates for mathematical honours roughly in four classes ; and the same questions were not proposed to all the classes. It may be seen from historical passages contained in the first report that this system was at last abandoned, and the principle adopted of giving the *same questions* to every candidate. It seems that we may take it as the result of. the experience of many examiners that the later method was the most advantageous for ascertaining the relative merits of the candidates; and thus it would appear that there ought to be no recurrence to the older method unless for the most obvious and cogent reasons.

In the first Report a sentence is quoted from a still older document, recommending that "there be not contained in any paper more questions than students well prepared have generally been found able to answer within the time allowed for such purpose." This precept is still, it may be presumed, theoretically binding; but its practical inefficiency may be seen from the fact that a Senior Wrangler usually obtains only about half the full number of marks : that is to say the papers are about twice as long as they should be in order to satisfy the prescribed condition. The sentence is reproduced in the regulations for the system which is to commence in 1873; and I earnestly hope that it will be regarded, and consequently the papers reduced to about half their present extent. At the same time I have had little confidence as to the matter; for the range of the subjects is to be so much wider for the future than it has been hitherto, that I can well understand how examiners in their natural desire to include every thing, easily yield to the temptation to crowd their papers with work which it would require superhuman power to perform.

In the first Report a sentence occurs which although definitely applied to a particular point involves a very

important principle. In the Regulations it was prescribed that the subject of Optics was to be treated
geometrically in the first three days, and the Board
held that under this order a strictly geometrical method
ought to be used. Then it is added : "At the same
time, taking into consideration that the attention of
the candidates to geometrical reasoning is sufficiently
secured by other subjects of examination in the first
three days, they are of opinion that with reference
to Optics, the restriction 'geometrically' may with advantage be omitted." The principle here brought forward is I think very valuable, namely, that after a
sufficient amount of training in a particular kind of
exercise, it is advisable to supply another instead of
prolonging that which has served its purpose.

In the Report of 1850, we find this sentence : "The
proof of the theorem that equations with rational coefficients are always resolvable into simple or quadratic
factors may be simply read to be understood, but not
to be produced in examination." The remark points to
a defect in our system of examination which seems to
me very grave. Take the proposition here cited,
namely, in substance, that every rational algebraical
equation has a root. The treatment of this proposition
by Cauchy is a very remarkable piece of modern analysis ; but it may be considered too long to set in an
examination, and hence it will probably be neglected by
students ; for to recommend them to read what is certain not to be required would be in general useless
advice. A valuable question might be formed by asking a student to give an analysis of the proof; but
unfortunately this exercise could not be very often or

T.   14

very extensively applied. For the result would be, that the students would be trained by their tutors to write out a prescribed form of analysis ; so that instead of the power of thought and expression we should have only that of memory cultivated and rewarded.

With one more extract from the Reports, I will conclude ; we read in that for 1860: "The Moderators regret that they must again call the attention of the Board to the very imperfect manner in which the questions in Elementary Astronomy were answered by the great majority of those who attempted them. This defect appeared to arise not so much from ignorance as from the want of the faculty of expression in treating a subject which perhaps more than any other requires the rare power of setting forth complicated geometrical conceptions in clear and popular language." I quote these remarks for the purpose of recording my entire concurrence with them. I do not know any part of our examination which has been treated with more judgment and skill than Elementary Astronomy ; but I fear that the candidates have rarely done justice to the questions proposed.

I would strongly recommend the study of the Reports for 1849 and 1850 to those who are interested in mathematical studies and examinations. The subjects are discussed with great moderation and judgment by very distinguished men, whose experience was recent of the examinations which they had endured and of those which they had conducted. It is much to be regretted that some of the most eminent of these should, about twenty years afterwards, have maintained apparently on theoretical grounds opinions directly contrary to those which they had originally derived from actual practice.

Now what conclusions ought to be maintained as to the success or failure of the Mathematical Examinations at Cambridge during the present generation? It would be presumptuous in me to express a positive opinion; it will be sufficient to offer some remarks which may assist those who wish to form an accurate judgment.

Probably in one respect the system of examinations might be strongly supported by a reference to the scientific position of some of the high wranglers. It is certainly curious that, to keep within the limits of our professorial body, we have no less than four senior wranglers; and it is obvious that our scientific staff is beyond comparison stronger than that of any other scientific institution in England. It is also evident that among the college and private tutors we have many persons who have taken high places in the examinations; in fact all the important mathematical instruction of the place, professional and voluntary, is conducted by teachers who have distinguished themselves in the Tripos.

It must in fairness be added, that as might have been expected those who have gained scientific reputation in addition to their academical success, belong mainly to the earlier period of the present generation; thus the four professors to whom I have alluded, passed their examinations before the period which commenced in 1847.

It would appear however from various circumstances that disappointment has been felt as to our system, and that this has been for some time gradually increas-

14—2

ing. The nature of the defects which may be charged
on any system must depend necessarily on the ideal we
form of the design of the system. Many persons seem
to hold that the great function of an examination is the
supply of a continued stream of eminent mathematicians ; and hence we find that a distinction is drawn
between what a high wrangler is supposed to be and
what it is assumed that he ought to be. Such words as the
following are based on this notion : "Merely to be able
to integrate, to solve differential equations, to work the
hardest of Senate House Problems &c. &c., is *not* to be
a mathematician. To deserve the name a man must
have some of the creative faculty, must be the ποιητὴς
if ever so little." I venture to disagree with what is
here said and implied. I take the list of accomplish-
ments which is recorded only to be depreciated, and
even omitting the &c. &c. by which it may be presumed
the list is augmented and intensified, I say that the
man who possesses these *is* a mathematician. He may
never have the leisure which official dignity and emoluments ensure, he may be shut out from every academical
advantage on account of his father's creed, he may be
compelled to occupy his time in constant drudgery for
the sake of subsistence, or he may devote his ability to
objects of deeper than scientific interest ; for all these
reasons he may contribute little to the advancement of
the subjects which he is qualified to handle, but he is
potentially a mathematician. We may illustrate two
of the points to which allusion has been made.

The same year which records the great name of Herschel at the head of the Tripos, preserves a little lower
down that of one who had left the weaver's bench only

a few months before he entered the University. The tradition has been preserved by some well qualified to judge, that if fortune had been more propitious both the academical honour and the ultimate scientific fame of the poorer candidate would not have been inferior to that of the great senior wrangler himself.

Or again are we to refuse to admit the mathematical ability of one who renounced all University distinction and prospects for the labour of a missionary in South Africa?

I do not think that any competent judge can be acquainted with the young men who emerge year after, year from our examinations and deny their claim to be called mathematicians, just because circumstances may not enable them to devote their future lives to the subject. Not a single educational appointment for which mathematical knowledge is a requisite is ever vacant without drawing forth well qualified Cambridge candidates, and one of them usually obtains the post. In fact the process may be laborious and costly, but there can be no doubt that our Cambridge examinations do furnish an ample supply of well trained and able mathematicians.

However quite apart from the opinions which may be formed outside the University there is apparently much dissatisfaction even among ourselves as to our present condition. Perhaps some of the reasons for this dissatisfaction may be assigned.

Probably the older notion that mathematics should be regarded by our students mainly as a discipline, and not as an end, still lingers among us: and consequently regret and disappointment may be felt because our high wranglers do not manifest the value of their training in the ordinary pursuits of life. To take an example often brought forward : it is said that in former times the judges and other great ornaments of the law were frequently Cambridge men - who had distinguished themselves at the University ; while now the mathematical tripos can scarcely find a good representative among the chiefs of the profession. Not only so, but medicine and theology formerly obtained distinguished cultivators from among the high wranglers, but scarcely ever now.

Moreover the college tutors cannot fail to notice a gradual decline in the attention and interest which candidates for high places in the mathematical tripos give to other branches of education. Attendance at lectures and examinations on classical and kindred subjects was formerly compulsory on all students ; practically such compulsion seems now to have ceased. I do not think it could be justly said that the highest men in the mathematical tripos are untrained in other and important matters ; but I may suggest that even they must suffer from an almost exclusive devotion to the studies in which they hope to excel. And for those of inferior ability who must, if possible, exhibit a still more laborious attention to their single pursuit, the disadvantageous consequences can hardly be avoided.

Probably with some observers there is an impression that we overwork our candidates for distinction. On glancing at the lists of very high wranglers for the last twenty years various painful cases present themselves of apparent exhaustion and premature death. It may be that these losses are not greater than some law of averages might have suggested; but this is not known, while the fact that careers which promised to be so bright have been clouded or extinguished, impresses us with obvious force.

Nor are there wanting direct testimonies, or at least strong opinions, as to the exhaustion produced by our long and fierce examination contests. An eminent member of the University recently brought to my notice the complaints of a celebrated conveyancer, that while his Cambridge pupils exhibited decisive evidence of training and of power, they shewed also too clearly that the training had been excessive, and the energy prematurely wasted. I have also heard a distinguished medical professor, with the best opportunity of judging, complaining in the most decided language of the exhaustion produced in the most promising students by our numerous, severe, and protracted examinations. That the competition is most severe becomes obvious on the slightest inspection of the circumstances. Schoolmasters seem to be on the watch for promising students who may be trained for the preliminary examinations. Colleges in the same University vie with each other, and one University strives with the other to secure the best material for supporting their credit. After years of assiduous cultivation before entering the University, followed by years of still more watchful treatment here, the candidates are brought to the contest which is almost to decide their future position in life.

Perhaps the dissatisfaction with our present system may be resolved almost entirely into the two components which I have noticed. There are in fact those who consider it to be the business of the University mainly to evolve a perennial supply of eminent mathematicians; and who assume that the supply is insufficient or unsatisfactory. I do not stay now to investigate the soundness of the notion thus held of the function of the University; nor even to ask if the results furnished are not fully equal to the demand for them. On the other hand there are those who consider mathematics as a valuable discipline, but believe and regret that at present we pursue them not on this ground, but almost exclusively as an end in themselves.

While I write I am directed to a newspaper criticism on the Cambridge Mathematical Tripos. The writer doubts whether the intense, incessant, and all-absorbing devotion to mathematics which even a tolerable place in the list of wranglers implies, is on the whole the best thing for the general strength and constitution of the mind. He says " with some striking exceptions the number of senior wranglers who have achieved subsequent greatness is not large." The words seem to suggest that the writer viewed mathematics mainly as a discipline, and not .as an end in themselves : and when he complains that few senior wranglers have subsequently distinguished themselves, he probably means that few of them now become famous in other pursuits.

Although I believe that our high wranglers are in general good mathematicians yet I must not be understood to affirm that the best mathematician is in all cases certainly at the top of the list, or that exceptional mathematical power is necessarily guaranteed by a high place in the Tripos. In all examinations, especially in those which are long and severe, the influence of secondary causes must be felt. Good health, sound nerves, and self possession play an important part; even expeditious writing is an element of advantage. Moreover one person may excel in invention and another in learning; one may be rapid but occasionally inaccurate, another slow but almost infallible; hence it is quite possible that some other system of examination might place the candidates in slightly different relative positions, and yet the general principle may be fully established that the high places are secured by men who possess decided mathematical taste and power.

But let us proceed to consider the last changes which have been effected in our examinations. As we have stated there was dissatisfaction felt both by those who regarded mathematical science as a discipline, and by those who regarded it as a profession; the latter seem to have been the most eager in expressing their opinion, and the most influential in carrying it into operation. About six years since two eminent scientific persons, not resident in the University, drew attention to the subject. One of them wrote a letter which was not published, but was brought under the notice of the Mathematical Board. In this letter certain important mathematical subjects were named as wholly or partially deficient in our examinations; and it was suggested that this might be owing to the ignorance of the examiners respecting them. The writer seemed to have overlooked the fact that some of these subjects had been expressly omitted by University regulations guided by the highest official authority; nor did he consider that examiners would scarcely be justified in departing from the established traditions and elevating into importance subjects which were within the range but were not made specially prominent. In fact in constructing an hypothesis to account for alleged defects in an examination paper it is unjust to have recourse to the ignorance of the examiners until every allowance has been made for the restraining conditions under which they act.

In consequence of the complaints thus urged against the current system a committee of distinguished mathematicians was appointed to consider the matter; and after long discussion they presented a report to the Senate of the University by which the scheme of examination was reconstructed. Some changes were made in the proposed scheme owing to strong objections which were expressed in discussion and in print; and finally it was adopted by a small majority.

It would not be advisable to enter into details which would be of little interest away from Cambridge, and almost superfluous there. We may say that the examination was again lengthened: it was proposed that $9\frac{1}{2}$ days should be the extent, but it appeared that the forbearance of the University would not tolerate this, and so nine days were taken. Then as to the range of subjects it may be said to include every thing, except perhaps quaternions. The first examination under the new system was to take place in 1873.

Speaking generally, the proposed alterations were advocated by the professors and some of the senior residents; but they were opposed by many who had obtained recent experience as teachers and examiners. For my own part I may say that I view the change with sorrow and dismay : it seems to me that the evils under which we suffer are aggravated without a single compensating advantage.

It is especially worthy of notice that the distinguished professors who twenty years before had recommended the omission of various subjects from the course on account of its great extent, at this time, without any obvious reason for the change, urged precisely the contrary. Moreover the earlier opinion was formed when the recollections of teaching and examination were still fresh ; the later opinion was given after a cessation of many years from practical familiarity with these matters. Out of the eleven principal supporters of the proposed system only one had been an examiner during the preceding 15 years, and the average period which had elapsed since they had examined was 22 years. Lastly, the majority of those who recommended an examination of $9\frac{1}{2}$ days had themselves fortunately escaped the eight days trial which had prevailed for a quarter of a century ; they had attained their academical distinctions after a struggle of six or even of five days. It may be natural that men who have become familiar with a subject by long and mature study should forget the labour and time they have expended on it, and thus be led to impose on mere youths a task beyond their strength ; but the result is an oppressive burden on those who have to endure the discipline.

As I have said, there was much opposition to the new system at Cambridge, and numerous valuable fly sheets were issued which well deserve attention. In the oral discussion of the subject much regret was expressed at the vehement competition which is characteristic of our proceedings. Some persons advocated the Oxford plan of putting the successful candidates in classes, and arranging each class alphabetically, instead of issuing a list in the so-called order of merit. It was objected that there might be a great disparity between the best and the worst members of a class, and thus it is unfair to place them apparently on a level. The reply was made that our present system is liable to the same kind of objection, inasmuch as two men occupying consecutive positions on the list may yet be separated by a very large number of marks, of which no public notice is ever given.

Let me now offer a few remarks on the system which is henceforward to prevail.

My first objection is that the examination is too long. The strain of nine days is, I hold, too great, and gives an undue advantage to mere physical strength. I am aware that many persons who have not undergone such a trial affirm confidently that it is not unreasonably severe. It is the longest examination which the University conducts; and probably few will deny that from the nature of the subjects the pressure is more severe than it would be in an examination of the same length in languages or in natural science.

I know there is a theory that the length of the examination can be rendered supportable, or even pleasant, if a few unoccupied days are interposed between its beginning and its end. Opinions vary as to the effect of such a suspense of work ; some candidates before trial anticipate relief from the arrangement, and a few from actual experience are in favour of it ; but many on the other hand obtain no practical benefit from the imposed pause, for it merely heightens and prolongs the torturing anxiety of the whole contest. The interval is too often spent in unwelcome recollections of past failures and errors, and in gloomy forebodings of the future ; and in general *they* will gain the least repose who have really undergone the greatest fatigue.

I can most distinctly say from my own experience as having encountered the eight days' examination, from having been much engaged as tutor of others under like circumstances, and from observation as an examiner, that the protracted labour and excitement of the examination does tell severely on candidates who are not of most robust strength. I feel confident that many fail to do themselves justice in the later papers, by reason of fatigue and exhaustion. We must not forget that the most important subjects, speaking generally, come latest in order in the examinations ; so that a candidate has the mortification of finding that his energies are declining just when there is the greatest need and the surest reward for their exertion.

It has sometimes occurred to me on perceiving the evident traces of fatigue and anxiety on the candidates towards the close of the trial, that it would be both kind and wise to reverse the order of the process, and set the most difficult papers first, so that they might be attacked with the freshest powers. It would be just as easy as at present to reject all those who quite failed in certain prescribed subjects.

But to consider the examinations in some detail. We are to have, in the first place, three days devoted to elementary subjects. This arrangement is held in considerable favour at Cambridge. A candidate is compelled to devote much attention to the earlier portions of the mathematical sciences ; unless he passes to the satisfaction of the examiners he cannot enter on the more advanced part of the examination. This arrangement has been borrowed from the Mathematical Tripos, where it originated, and is now adopted in the Natural Sciences and in the Classical Examinations. I apprehend that the great advantage of the arrangement is that it ensures the appearance of a large number of questions which men of moderate ability can try : it is, in fact, a kind of protection set up for them which prevents them from being completely sacrificed to the interests of the more eminent candidates. The merit which is sometimes claimed that a competent knowledge of the elementary subjects is thus secured is very uncertain, for in practice the standard below which a candidate must not fall will almost always be extremely moderate.

On the other hand, I think that this arrangement presses rather heavily on the candidates for the highest places. They are compelled to pay great attention to the subjects which are set in the earlier days, for if they do not they cannot recover the lost ground during the rest of the examination. But the nature of the subjects is such that it may be doubted if the labour spent on them is duly repaid by the advantage which it brings. Take, for example, Geometrical Conic Sections. The candidate must commit to memory a large number of isolated demonstrations, not only of different propositions, but even of the same proposition, if he wishes to be fully prepared for his trial. Again, take the three sections of Newton. Many of the propositions depend on special artifices, and although it may be a valuable exercise to study and understand them, it does not follow that there is any great benefit in committing them to memory. The burden falls most heavily on the best men, because they have also to keep in their heads, as they best can, all the formulæ and methods required for the higher subjects which are to follow. This is one of the ways in which our examination system presses severely on the most promising candidates; tending to exhaust them before the opportunity arrives for them really to display their powers.

Now let us pass to the next part of the examination, which consists of six days devoted to the higher mathematical subjects. These subjects are arranged in five groups, and provision is made for each group to receive a proper amount of attention. Ten bookwork papers and two problem papers are to be given to cover the whole ground.

Now two courses were possible. It might have been supposed that no candidate would take in all the groups of subjects; and so papers might have been set containing far more questions than any single candidate could answer in the prescribed time. The advantage of the course is that by this means a very large number of questions might be set; and so each subject not inadequately represented. The disadvantage would be that a candidate who might possibly know every thing could not bring all that knowledge into evidence ; and moreover owing to the wide choice offered to them candidates would practically be working at different papers, and so an accurate comparison of their merits would be difficult.

The other course which was possible was adopted, and stated in these words : " The same Questions shall be proposed throughout the Examination to all the Candidates ; and there shall not be contained in any Paper more Questions than Students well prepared in all the subjects may be expected to answer within the time allowed for that Paper." The disadvantage is that the range of mathematical learning is so wide that it seems impossible to represent it under these conditions within the eight book-work papers. There are thirty-seven subjects included by name in the five groups. It is true that in some cases a subject is separated into two, a higher and a lower part ; but then on the other hand under some titles we find matter which is well capable of division. Take for example *Heat :* it may be fairly maintained that three distinct and important subjects are thus suggested, each of which is developed in well known books. We have the experimental facts and laws, the theory of conduction, and the mechanical theory :· moreover there are not inconsiderable diversities in the modes of treating each of these subjects ; for example the theory of conduction may be studied in the earlier analysis of Fourier and Poisson, or according to the more recent method of Lamé.

Now since the old regulation is revived and apparently to be enforced that no more is to be proposed in any paper than a well prepared student can answer, and bearing in mind that at present a senior wrangler

may gain about half marks on an average, it follows
that the current length of the papers should be about
halved. Hence it appears that on an average a single
question only can be allotted to each of the thirty-
seven distinct heads under which mathematical science
is arranged.

This seems a fatal difficulty ; it is scarcely possible
to do justice to the subjects with such a small supply
of questions. Take for instance *Elliptic Integrals.*
This consists of numerous long and difficult investigations, conducted in many cases by highly artificial
methods. A single question may very easily be badly
treated by a candidate, or may be almost forgotten,
and yet he may have a reasonable knowledge of the
whole subject. If however the examiners are restricted
by custom, or by enactment to a few selected propositions, an objection of another kind arises. Every candidate who aims at a high place will learn these propositions by heart ; and there will be no criterion by
which to distinguish between the rival performances.

I do but repeat a remark which I have already
made when I say that out of the large mass of mathematical science displayed before our candidates there is
much which is ill adapted for examination purposes, as
consisting principally of a heavy weight on the memory.
To illustrate the point from an elementary subject take
the first proposition in Newton's second section ; this is
a most valuable and favourable specimen of his methods :
when once *understood* it may be considered *known*, for it
can be produced with little effort, in a reasonably accurate
form, whenever it is required. Both in an educational
and in an examinational point of view the proposition

is highly valuable. But now compare with this some of the propositions which follow in the second and third sections as to the laws of force in assigned orbits, for instance in an ellipse round a force in the focus : these investigations are collections of geometrical artifices which must be laboriously committed to memory, and retained by constant exercise, in order to be ready at the examiner's call. In the higher departments of mathematics there are whole subjects which are unsuited for an examiner's operations, though intrinsically of great value. Take for example, the *Figure of the Earth*, which is of the highest interest historically and theoretically, and has been the fertile source of many striking improvements in mathematics ; from its nature it offers little scope for the exercises and the deductions which examinations demand. Any important variation in the course of the investigation would find an appropriate place in a mathematical memoir, but not in a question to be discussed in twenty minutes by an anxious candidate at an examination. Under our present system the subject forms a severe task even for a tenacious memory.

But now let us advert to another examination which the candidates for the highest mathematical honours are called to undergo; I mean the Smith's Prizes Examinations.

It will be remembered that we left our candidates at the end of nine days severe work. A week elapses during which the examiners settle the merits of the candidates. Then commences another examination of four or five days for the two annual prizes founded by Dr Smith to be awarded to "the best proficients in

Mathematics and Natural Philosophy." About six or eight of the highest wranglers usually present themselves for this additional trial.

It is almost impossible to find at the present day any pretence at justification for this examination, which professes to be to determine the best proficients in Mathematics and Natural Philosophy. It is conceivable that at the time of the foundation of the prize other subjects might have been mixed up with mathematics in the examination which fixed the places of the wranglers, and the senior and junior optimes, so that success was not due solely to mathematical attainments. But at the present time no such foreign element disturbs the purity of the first verdict. The University constructs an elaborate machinery for theoretically discovering the best mathematician: this machinery is to be worked for nine days by five skilful engineers, and the results are to be published. Immediately after this operation, a new process is instituted for obtaining the same result quite independently of all that has been already effected. The absurdity of the transaction will be seen best by imagining a parallel case. The University has lately instituted various new Triposes; for example one for proficiency in the Natural Sciences, administered by five examiners. This Tripos then arranges in order of merit annually the students of Natural Sciences, according to the best scheme which the University can devise and execute. Suppose that a person were to found an annual prize for the best proficient in Natural Science; surely the University must consistently with its own plans award the prize to the first person in the Natural Science

Tripos; it would be suicidal to affirm that the elaborate apparatus for arranging the students in order of merit already employed was worthless, and the results an illusion; so that the process required not to be supplemented merely by a prolonged investigation, but to be replaced by a perfectly distinct operation.

Even if it could be suggested that the examination for the Mathematical Tripos was good so far as it went, but that it was incomplete, this would not justify the system of a second independent examination. The most that could be reasonably maintained is that some prolongation of the trial was necessary; and then the final award of the Smith's Prizes ought to be made on the joint decision of the two sets of examiners. In other words, the moderators and examiners of the Senate House should have their votes as well as the special examiners for the Smith's Prizes; and the judgment be settled by the majority of votes. Some such plan would, I think, be a great improvement on the present practice. The whole evidence would then be employed in guiding the decision; whereas at present, when the prizes are assigned solely from the results of the second examination, the evidence which is neglected is probably superior in quality to that which is accepted, and is certainly more than double in quantity.

I have implied that in my opinion the examination for the Smith's Prizes taken singly is not so trustworthy as that for the Mathematical Tripos. The reasons for this opinion may now be stated.

1. The Tripos Examination is longer, and therefore more varied and searching.

2. The papers for the Tripos examination seem

to be constructed with far more elaborate care than those for the Smith's Prizes Examination; it would be scarcely too much to say that as many months are spent in preparation for the former as of days for the latter. The papers for the Tripos Examination are submitted to the criticism of all the staff engaged on the work. Moreover, the marks for each question are assigned on the judgment of all. This is a most valuable precaution. For, in the first place, a more accurate estimate of the value of a problem will frequently be given by his colleagues whom he consults than the constructor of the problem could himself form. Moreover, by the consultation of the examiners it may be pretty well settled whether a particular question is likely to be naturally suggested by some book or manuscript in circulation in the University, or whether it would present itself as a complete novelty. This is a most important element in determining the value to be assigned to a solution; and I can say from experience that great errors might and would be made in this respect by a person ill informed as to the sources of knowledge accessible to the students. In the Senate House, where a large number of candidates is presented to notice, an examiner will sometimes be warned by the circumstance of several persons sending up a solution in nearly the same manner that the problem is not new. But in the Smith's Prizes Examination, where the candidates are much fewer, it is not at all impossible for a solution to be submitted to the examiner which has nothing original about it, and yet it may be estimated as a new and independent investigation.

In short, the examiners for the Smith's Prizes do not secure that assistance in assigning value to individual questions, which is an important element in awarding merit to the candidates.

3. In the Tripos Examination the places are determined by the aggregate of the marks obtained. It is generally understood that in the Smith's Prizes Examination each examiner *votes* for the two candidates whom he thinks best. It is obvious that by this method two examiners whose papers, by accident or reason, are of very unequal value and importance; may exercise equal influence on the decision. It is conceivable that if the decision rested with a single examiner he might be able to deliver his opinion without having made use of marks; but if more than one examiner is engaged, it seems difficult to suppose that a satisfactory result can be obtained unless marks are used, and combined, after having been reduced by some means to a uniform scale.

4. It must be remembered that the candidates enter on the second examination soon after the fatigue and excitement of one of the severest trials to which students can be exposed: this alone would render the results suspicious. Then it is evident that the pressure of the second examination falls very unequally on the candidates. The senior wrangler has everything to lose, and practically nothing to gain. If he secures the first Smith's Prize it adds little to the honour he has already gained; but if he fails the loss of reputation is most decided and serious. The second wrangler, on the one hand, may gain, inasmuch as he may displace the senior wrangler, and, on the other

hand, he may lose by the promotion of one of the lower wranglers. But the lower wranglers are themselves in a much more satisfactory position; they stake nothing, and they may gain immensely. It would be but fair to make a rule that these circumstances should be regarded in awarding the Smith's Prizes, and that no revolution should be permitted in the order already fixed by the Tripos Examination unless the propriety of it should be most signally demonstrated.

But we must in justice allude to some of the arguments which may be urged to vindicate the importance of the Smith's Prizes Examination, and its superiority to the Tripos Examination.

1. The Smith's Prizes Examination is conducted by the Mathematical Professors; and it may be supposed that it must in consequence necessarily excel all that can be accomplished by men generally junior in years, and far inferior in academic position. It will be acknowledged as most obvious that the leisure, the dignity, and the emoluments of the University professorships enable their occupants to acquire knowledge far superior in amount and in quality to that which is likely to be possessed by any mere scientific amateur. And hence naturally the works of the Professors will far surpass those of the ordinary members of the University in influence and extent, in accuracy and erudition. But it does not follow necessarily that the Professors will also be the most skilful examiners. On the one hand, the higher researches in which the Professors are naturally occupied do not always yield an abundant supply of the material which can be used in examinations; they are too difficult and too long

to be cut up conveniently into questions of moderate length. And on the other hand, Examination, like every other pursuit and profession, is an employment in which excellence is obtained by prolonged experience : now in mathematical examinations, and the cognate function of mathematical instruction, the training of the Tripos examiners may very often exceed that of the Professors.

2. It is sometimes claimed as a merit for the Smith's Prizes Examination that as rather more time is allowed for each paper speed of action tells less than in the Senate House. It may be replied in the first place that the evil of tempestuous haste ought to be removed from the Tripos Examination, and not tolerated there in order to contrast with the serene calm of the Smith's Prizes contest. And in the second place that the assumed relative advantage does not exist, because although more time may be allowed for a paper in the later examinations, yet the paper may be more than proportionably difficult.

3. It is asserted that the papers in the later examination are different in character from those of the earlier set, and sometimes it is added that they are more philosophical, whatever that may happen to mean. The answer is that those who by virtue of their occupations may be said to be professional observers of examination papers, testify that they do not perceive the difference nor admit the claimed superiority. The Smith's Prizes papers are perhaps on the whole more difficult, but this cannot be considered an advantage, for those in the Tripos Examination are scarcely easy enough.

It has been stated that the chief value of the Smith's Prizes Examination consists in the "opportunity it affords for distinction to those students who have of their own accord directed their reading more especially towards scientific objects and researches." This implies most obviously that there are two classes of subjects in our examination, the scientific and the unscientific; and the remedy would seem to be to rearrange our schedule, and omit all the less valuable portions. In other words, if there be a difference in character in the two examinations let the better be selected and adopted and the other discontinued.

While the Senate House Examination was limited so as to exclude some branches of mathematics there might be a faint excuse for a second trial which should extend over the omitted portions. But now that the Senate House Examination is to include everything even this faint excuse is obliterated.

In discussing the relative merits of the Tripos Examination and the Smith's Prizes Examination we may appeal to evidence to corroborate the opinion which we have endeavoured to support by argument.

1. We may adduce the important testimony of the late Mr Hopkins, the well known eminent mathematical tutor. He published a paper on the subject in which he maintained that when the Smith's Prizes Examiners abandoned the decision of the Senate House Examiners, they were wrong three times out of four.

2. We may recall the fact that about twelve years since the Council of the University recommended almost unanimously the extinction of the Smith's Prizes

Examinations, and the employment of the funds for the purposes of a Prize Essay.

3. The circumstance is worthy of notice that among the members of the body by which the scheme henceforth to prevail was drawn up, if we exclude the Smith's Prizes examiners, there was a decided majority in favour of the extinction of the examination.

In concluding, one inconsistency may be observed among the proceedings of some of the strenuous upholders of the Smith's Prizes Examinations. They have constructed and induced the University to adopt a scheme for the Tripos Examinations which is extremely minute and particular in its provisions; at the same time they leave the Smith's Prizes Examination without any rule whatever at the simple discretion of those who conduct it : then they maintain the merit and even the superiority of the later examination. That is an elaborate plan has been traced out while at the same time it is practically asserted that action unfettered by any plan is best. The consequence seems to me a great confusion and contradiction in theory. For example, under the new regulations a provision is made to secure the equable flow of certain streams of subjects into the Tripos Examination, in order that the student may guide his reading so as to secure the greatest payment for his ability and application. But there is no corresponding provision with respect to the Smith's Prizes ; so that if a candidate has made a judicious choice of a division and gained distinction thereby in the Tripos, he may be involved in disaster if the examiners do not represent that division adequately in the later contest.

It must be admitted that suggestions have been made with the view of ameliorating the evils connected with the Smith's Prizes Examination, but not apparently with any striking success. One such suggestion has been to postpone the examination until a year after the Senate House Examination. An obvious objection is that this practically amounts to assigning the prizes to the wealthy candidates who can afford to continue their training during another year, excluding the poorer candidates who must begin to work for their living. Moreover this suggestion does not in any way diminish the evils which are connected with the multiplication of examinations, and with the unsuitableness of the higher branches of mathematics for these competitive struggles.

The professors themselves seem to consider that a great improvement is effected by setting a paper of subjects for essays; it is however difficult to admit that this is any real benefit. Several subjects are proposed in order to secure some choice; and thus the perplexity arises of attempting to compare the merits of two essays on totally different matters. It was well said during the last controversy on examinations that it is "idle to attempt to balance one man's Elliptic Integrals against another's Elastic Solids." In fact if all the candidates wrote on the same subject it would be easy to form a judgment of the comparative merit, and some conjecture might be hazarded as to the originality exhibited in the essays. But if each candidate selects his own subject, any evaluation of merit must be most precarious, from the dissimilarity of the things compared and the difficulty of ascertaining what is original and what is acquired.

I know of no remedy for the Smith's Prizes Examination except abolishing them; the institution seems to me to offer a good example of the principle affirmed by many political economists, that all endowments require periodical inspection in order to determine if they are discharging any good functions. Dr Smith was doubtless a man of blameless character and eminent ability; and yet I believe that his benevolent design is now productive of a decided balance of mischief and misery. Perhaps we have an illustration in his Prizes of the well known caution that the virtues of men in high station are sometimes more dangerous than their vices.

I will venture to reproduce some remarks which I made in the discussion which took place in the University when the new scheme was proposed. Are our students so buoyant after they have obtained their degrees that we can reproach ourselves with having left their craving for work unsatisfied, their energies unemployed? The opinion of many I believe is quite the reverse; they hold that we destroy the elasticity of our students by the incessant toil of examinations, that we squander with lavish prodigality the fresh energy of youth and early manhood, and suffer too often retribution in the languor and unprofitableness of maturer life. Let us appeal to observation. The examination has been extended from 5 days to 6; then from 6 to 8, and now it is to be drawn out to 9 days, and the demand may be distinctly heard for more time still. In the course of one generation the duration has been nearly doubled, and the severity much more than doubled. A promising undergraduate of the period would probably smile at the problems which were proposed to such men as Herschel and Peacock and Whewell; but can we flatter ourselves that by our elaborate machinery for examinations we produce men superior to our academical ancestors for the pursuits of active or of studious life? The question has been implied in an able fly-sheet: Are our modern University men better Divines, better Lawyers, better Mathematicians, better Philosophers than those of the preceding generation?

Some surprise was expressed at Cambridge at the date of the discussion, at finding the new scheme supported by the approbation of two distinguished Professors of Natural Philosophy in Northern Universities. There was, in fact, the obvious fallacy that these distinguished philosophers recommended to others a course very different from that which they adopted themselves. They devote their energies to teaching, and their pupils are not crushed with severe examinations; but for us without any exhortation to improved instruction they prescribed increased examinations. It is curious that one of these persons, whose influence helped to render the burden more grievous at Cambridge, has since declared himself strenuously hostile to all competitive examinations.

On the other hand, two private letters reached me at the time which deserved, I think, even more weight than the opinions of the eminent northern professors to whom I have just alluded, because the writers, who were adverse to the proposed changes, were practically familiar with the subject. One was from the late Professor De Morgan. He spoke of two proposed *alterations*, which he thought would prove *aggravations;* and said : " Hamilton of Edinburgh called Cambridge a slaughter-house of intellect. Looking at him as an historian I should not agree with him ; but taking him as a prophet, I do not know what to say."

The other letter was from a member of the University, who had but recently gained the highest mathematical honours, and entered on a course of original research of the fairest promise; it spoke in the strongest terms of the dismay which would naturally fill the minds of students in future as they looked at the boundless field of subjects which they would have to explore for examination purposes.

The difference in opinion as to the last changes at Cambridge may be not unfairly summed up as a contest between those who desired more instruction and those who recommended severer examinations ; the latter party unfortunately, in my opinion, was victorious. Since that period circumstances have drawn increased attention to the functions and the ideal of an endowed University ; and perhaps we are on the eve of improvements. There appear to be three distinct functions which are recognised as pertaining to the University : one is that of examination, one that of teaching, one that of fostering original research. The first of these three has practically been as yet most regarded ; and many of us hope that it will in future decline either absolutely or relatively by the increased

development of the other two. As to the matter of
original research, without asserting that this is adequately regarded, yet we may say that there has been
much improvement in recent times. The professorships have in various cases been augmented from some
convenient funds, and thus elevated above the misera-
ble pittances of which they formerly consisted; while
the permission to retain a fellowship with them, notwithstanding marriage, has indirectly been a great
boon to them. Moreover, many of the colleges have
now the power to confer a fellowship on any person
eminent in science and learning; and thus there is at
least the opportunity, in cases where the will also
exists, to encourage and assist those who devote themselves to unremunerative intellectual pursuits.

But it seems to me that the most decided want in
the place is an organised system of scientific instruction; and this remains although it would appear that
various efforts have been made to supply the defect.
For more than a quarter of a century the entire range
of mixed mathematics has been represented in University public instruction by courses annually delivered
on Astronomical Instruments, Lunar Theory, Hydrostatics and Optics. Statutes have been drawn up with
a view to secure the due distribution of the "various
branches of mathematical science on which it is desirable that lectures should be given:" and the duty of
carrying the statutes into effect has been assigned to
the Mathematical Board. The want of a suitable
building and collection of instruments has been held to
constitute the great obstacle to University instruction.

The building however has been erected, and some advance made towards the formation of a collection of instruments. However the phantom of a well arranged and extensive cycle of public instruction seems still to elude the grasp; instead of it we have ever augmenting examinations. If there is no existing staff to which this public instruction can be assigned one should be forthwith called into existence, with due provision for effective work and reasonable remuneration.

Even if scientific lectures were not properly appreciated there still remains another mode of instruction which ought to be adopted, and which would perhaps be still more valuable than oral teaching; I mean the publication of works on the higher branches of mathematics which should combine, correct and illustrate what has been scattered through the Transactions of Societies and the articles of scientific journals. I do not allude to mere academical compendia, of which in general there is a sufficient supply, but to works treating elaborately and fully the highest subjects. The history of science offers us splendid examples of such works; the *Mécanique Céleste* itself is one of them. For modern instances I may refer to the writings of Lamé, Chasles, Serret, Helmholtz and Clebsch: these men are eminent not only as original investigators and oral teachers, but as the authors of noble treatises. It will be highly advantageous if those who hold appointments which secure leisure for research will accept it as a duty to compose one systematic work at least of the kind now indicated; it may be safely said that the result will do more for the advancement of science than the production of matter which is merely entombed in the memoirs of learned bodies. Amateurs may in some cases attempt to execute such tasks, but it is obvious that owing to the little leisure they can secure from their necessary avocations they must fall far below the standard which the professional cultivators of science can attain.

The views which I have endeavoured to enforce may be summed up thus :

Instead of making our mathematical examinations longer and harder they ought to be made shorter and easier.

The cultivation of the higher branches of mathematics pure and mixed may be promoted not so much by severe examinations as by professional teaching, oral and printed ; and in this the University is lamentably deficient.

But I cannot conclude without especially stating what is implied in many of my remarks ; I wish to join my protest, feeble as it may be, with that of many other persons both within and without the University, against the exorbitant development of the system of competitive examinations. We assume in all our arrangements that men will read only what will pay in examinations, and assume it I believe contrary to the evidence furnished by other Universities, and by our own : and by shewing how firmly we grasp this sordid creed ourselves we do our best to recommend it to others. We give our highest honours and rewards for success in special examinations ; and thus we practically encourage not the harmonious development of

T.   16

all the faculties of the mind, but the morbid growth of some and the decay of others. We tempt our students to regard degrees and fellowships as the end of life, and not as incentives to manly exertion and aids to pure unselfish service; we cannot wonder then that not a few who start in their course so well seem to fail : to use Bacon's simile, they resemble the fabled Atalanta who lost the race because she stooped to pick up the golden apples.

CAMBRIDGE : PRINTED BY C. J. CLAY, M.A. AT THE UNIVERSITY PRESS.

For EU product safety concerns, contact us at Calle de José Abascal, 56–1°,
28003 Madrid, Spain or eugpsr@cambridge.org.